The Velocity Banking Mortgage Payoff Method

How to Use Cash Flow, Lines of Credit, and Strategic Payments to Eliminate Debt Faster

By Joseph G. Correa

Copyright & Legal Notice

Published by Live Stronger Faster

First Edition, 2026

Table of Contents

Introduction 5

Chapter 1: The Foundation of Velocity Banking — Understanding Cash Flow, Interest, and Financial Acceleration.......................13

Chapter 2: How Interest Really Works — Why Most Homeowners Stay in Debt for Decades...28

Chapter 3: The Power of Cash Flow — Why Income Management Matters More Than Income Size..43

Chapter 4: Understanding HELOCs and Revolving Credit — The Core Tools Behind Velocity Banking...59

Chapter 5: The Chunking Strategy — Using Strategic Lump-Sum Payments to Destroy Mortgage Principal Faster......................72

Chapter 6: The Role of Discipline and Financial Behavior — Why Velocity Banking Fails for Some People..................................86

Chapter 7: Building the Velocity Banking System — Step-by-Step Implementation for Real Life..100

Chapter 8: The Risks of Velocity Banking — What Every Homeowner Must Understand Before Starting....................... 110

Chapter 9: Combining Velocity Banking with Investing — Building Wealth While Accelerating Debt Payoff.....................121

Chapter 10: The Ultimate Velocity Banking Blueprint — Integrating Everything into a Complete Financial System........132

Final Tips and Suggestions for Mortgage Freedom...................141

Introduction

Debt can either become a lifelong burden or a powerful financial tool depending on how it is managed. For most homeowners, the mortgage is the largest debt they will ever carry. Traditional mortgage structures are designed to stretch repayment over decades, maximizing interest paid to the lender while minimizing financial flexibility for the borrower. Many homeowners faithfully make their monthly payments for years without realizing that the majority of those payments in the early years go toward interest rather than principal reduction. This system keeps millions of people trapped in long-term debt cycles, delaying wealth creation, retirement freedom, and financial independence. Yet there are advanced strategies that can dramatically accelerate mortgage payoff without requiring massive income increases or unrealistic sacrifices. One of the most powerful and misunderstood methods is the velocity banking mortgage payoff strategy.

Velocity banking is not magic, and it is not a loophole that eliminates debt overnight. Instead, it is a strategic cash flow management system designed to reduce interest expenses and improve the efficiency of every dollar you earn. When used correctly, this strategy can help homeowners reduce mortgage balances faster, shorten loan terms significantly, and free up cash flow that can later be redirected toward investing, business ownership, retirement accounts, or additional real estate opportunities. The goal of this book is to explain how velocity banking works in practical, understandable language so you can determine whether this strategy fits your financial goals, income structure, and risk tolerance.

At its core, velocity banking focuses on using cash flow strategically rather than passively. Most people deposit their income into a standard checking account, pay bills throughout the month, and allow leftover cash to sit idle or disappear through unnecessary spending. Meanwhile, interest on long-term debt continues accumulating daily. Velocity banking changes this process by repositioning available cash to attack debt more aggressively while simultaneously improving liquidity management. The strategy often involves the use of home equity lines of credit, revolving credit accounts, or other flexible borrowing tools combined with disciplined budgeting and structured payment systems.

One of the reasons velocity banking attracts so much attention is because it challenges traditional financial thinking. Many people are taught that all debt is dangerous and that financial success only comes from slowly making monthly payments over time. Others are told to aggressively pay down debt without considering cash flow flexibility or investment opportunities. Velocity banking introduces a more dynamic approach by recognizing that timing, cash movement, and interest efficiency matter. Instead of simply focusing on making larger mortgage payments, the strategy seeks to optimize how money flows through your financial system.

This book is not intended to encourage reckless borrowing or irresponsible financial behavior. In fact, velocity banking requires discipline, organization, and a deep understanding of your financial habits. Without proper structure, misuse of revolving credit can create financial stress instead of financial freedom. That is why this book emphasizes education first. You will learn not only the mechanics of velocity banking, but also the risks, limitations, misconceptions, and situations where the strategy may or may not be appropriate. Financial tools are neither good nor bad by themselves. Their effectiveness depends entirely on how they are used.

One of the biggest misconceptions surrounding velocity banking is the belief that it relies on “tricking the banks” or creating free money. This is completely false. Banks understand how revolving credit works and design products like home equity lines of credit to generate profit. The advantage for the borrower comes from using these products intelligently and strategically rather than emotionally or carelessly. The strategy works by reducing average daily interest accumulation and improving the speed at which debt principal is reduced. Small improvements in interest efficiency, when compounded over many years, can create significant financial benefits.

Another important concept introduced in this book is the relationship between liquidity and debt reduction. Many homeowners aggressively apply all extra cash toward their mortgage only to later face emergencies that force them into high-interest credit card debt or expensive personal loans. Velocity banking attempts to balance debt payoff with financial flexibility. Maintaining access to available credit and preserving liquidity can sometimes create greater long-term stability than simply eliminating debt as fast as possible without a broader strategy.

As you progress through this book, you will begin to see that velocity banking is really about financial behavior and systems management. Two people with identical incomes and identical mortgage balances can experience completely different financial outcomes based solely on how they manage their monthly cash flow. One person may remain trapped in debt for decades while another steadily reduces liabilities and builds wealth simultaneously. The difference often lies not in income level but in financial structure, planning, and consistency. This strategy becomes especially powerful for individuals with stable income, strong budgeting habits, and positive monthly cash flow. Business owners, self-employed individuals, commission-based earners, real estate investors, and high-income professionals often find velocity banking particularly attractive because they may have fluctuating cash flow patterns or excess monthly income that can be deployed strategically. However, even moderate-income households may benefit from aspects of the strategy when implemented carefully and conservatively.

A key tool commonly associated with velocity banking is the home equity line of credit, often referred to as a HELOC. Unlike a traditional mortgage that functions as a fixed installment loan, a HELOC operates as revolving credit secured by home equity. Interest is typically charged only on the outstanding balance, and funds can often be reused after repayment. This flexibility creates opportunities for strategic cash management when paired with disciplined financial habits. However, because a HELOC is secured by your home, improper use can create serious risks. Throughout this book, you will learn how to evaluate these risks responsibly.

You will also discover that velocity banking is not solely about paying off a mortgage early. The larger objective is creating financial acceleration. Once debt obligations decrease, the cash flow previously consumed by interest and monthly payments can be redirected toward wealth-building opportunities. This may include investing in retirement accounts, purchasing investment properties, funding businesses, building emergency reserves, or increasing overall financial security. In other words, mortgage payoff becomes part of a broader financial freedom strategy rather than an isolated goal.

Another critical lesson explored in this book is the importance of understanding interest calculations. Many homeowners do not realize how mortgage amortization schedules heavily favor lenders during the early years of repayment. Because interest is front-loaded, reducing principal earlier in the loan term can create disproportionately large savings over time. Velocity banking seeks to accelerate this process by reducing balances more aggressively and strategically than standard monthly payment structures typically allow.

This book will also address the emotional side of debt. Financial decisions are not purely mathematical. Fear, stress, insecurity, lifestyle pressure, and consumer habits often influence how people manage money. Some individuals feel anxious carrying any form of debt, while others become overconfident and misuse credit irresponsibly. A successful velocity banking strategy requires emotional discipline as much as financial knowledge. Understanding your personal financial behavior may ultimately determine your long-term success more than any spreadsheet or formula. You will encounter real-world examples, practical scenarios, and step-by-step concepts throughout this series. The goal is not to overwhelm you with complicated financial jargon but to provide practical education that can be applied in real life. Whether you are carrying a thirty-year mortgage, managing multiple debts, or seeking ways to accelerate financial freedom, the concepts in this book are designed to help you think differently about money management and mortgage strategy.

It is also important to understand that velocity banking is not universally recommended for everyone. Certain individuals may benefit more from traditional mortgage payoff methods, debt snowball strategies, refinancing, investment-focused approaches, or conservative budgeting systems. Your income stability, spending discipline, interest rates, emergency reserves, credit profile, and financial goals all play important roles in determining whether this strategy fits your situation. Throughout this book, you will learn how to evaluate these factors honestly and responsibly.

Financial freedom rarely comes from a single tactic. Instead, it comes from combining multiple intelligent strategies over time. The homeowners who build lasting wealth are often those who understand how to control cash flow, minimize unnecessary interest expenses, maintain financial flexibility, and deploy money strategically. Velocity banking can become one component of a larger wealth acceleration system when used wisely and carefully.

The purpose of this book is not to sell fantasy or unrealistic promises. Instead, it is to provide education, perspective, and practical tools that may help you take greater control of your financial future. By understanding how money moves, how interest accumulates, and how strategic payment systems operate, you can begin making more informed decisions about debt, cash flow, and long-term wealth creation.

The mortgage does not have to control your life for thirty years. With education, discipline, and intelligent financial systems, it may be possible to dramatically accelerate your path toward debt reduction and financial independence. The chapters ahead will guide you through the principles, strategies, calculations, risks, and implementation methods behind velocity banking so you can determine how to apply these concepts effectively within your own financial journey.

Chapter 1

The Foundation of Velocity Banking — Understanding Cash Flow, Interest, and Financial Acceleration

Most homeowners spend their lives focusing almost entirely on one number when it comes to their mortgage payment: the required monthly payment. They budget around it, organize their bills around it, and slowly accept the idea that the debt will remain with them for twenty, twenty-five, or even thirty years. Few stop to analyze how the mortgage system actually works, how interest accumulates, or how the timing of payments dramatically impacts the total cost of borrowing. Even fewer realize that their financial habits and cash flow management patterns often matter more than their income level alone. Before anyone can successfully use velocity banking, they must first understand the true foundation behind the strategy: the movement of cash flow and the mechanics of interest.

Traditional mortgages are structured using amortization schedules. In the early years of a mortgage, the majority of the monthly payment goes toward interest rather than principal reduction. This means many homeowners can make payments faithfully for years while barely reducing the actual loan balance. The bank benefits from time because the longer the loan exists, the more interest is collected. For example, a homeowner with a thirty-year mortgage may eventually pay hundreds of thousands of dollars in interest over the life of the loan depending on the interest rate and loan amount. Most people never fully realize how expensive time becomes when attached to long-term debt.

Velocity banking starts with the understanding that reducing principal faster reduces future interest accumulation. Interest is calculated based on the remaining balance. When principal decreases more aggressively, future interest calculations also decrease. This creates a compounding effect that works in favor of the borrower rather than exclusively benefiting the lender. The strategy revolves around accelerating the speed at which debt balances decline while maximizing the efficiency of available income and cash flow.

One of the most important principles in velocity banking is recognizing that money sitting idle often loses financial power. Many households allow their income to flow into a checking account where it remains inactive while mortgage interest continues accumulating daily. Velocity banking challenges this passive system by repositioning income to reduce debt balances more strategically. Instead of allowing money to remain idle, the strategy seeks to use cash flow continuously and efficiently.

To understand this concept more clearly, imagine two homeowners with identical mortgages, identical incomes, and identical monthly expenses. The first homeowner follows the standard financial routine. They receive a paycheck, deposit it into a checking account, make monthly payments, and save small leftover amounts. The second homeowner uses structured cash flow management by directing available income strategically toward reducing interest-bearing balances. Over time, the second homeowner may reduce debt substantially faster despite earning the exact same income. The difference lies not in earnings but in the movement and timing of money.

Velocity banking often incorporates revolving credit tools such as home equity lines of credit. Unlike traditional installment loans with fixed balances and fixed repayment structures, revolving credit allows funds to be borrowed, repaid, and reused repeatedly. Interest is generally charged only on the outstanding balance rather than the full credit limit. This flexibility creates opportunities for strategic debt acceleration when managed responsibly.

For example, if a borrower receives regular income deposits throughout the month, depositing that income into a revolving account temporarily reduces the average daily balance and therefore reduces interest accumulation. As bills are paid throughout the month, the balance fluctuates, but the average interest exposure may remain lower compared to leaving large balances untouched. Over time, this process may improve debt efficiency and accelerate payoff timelines.

The key to velocity banking is not borrowing more money endlessly. In fact, responsible implementation usually focuses on reducing total debt over time. The revolving account simply becomes a financial tool that improves cash flow efficiency and minimizes wasted interest expenses. However, without discipline, revolving credit can become dangerous. People who overspend, lack budgeting structure, or continuously increase liabilities may create larger financial problems instead of solving existing ones. That is why understanding behavior is just as important as understanding math.

One of the greatest financial weaknesses many households face is inconsistent cash flow management. People often spend emotionally rather than strategically. They increase expenses as income rises, rely heavily on consumer debt, and fail to maintain structured financial systems. Velocity banking requires the opposite mindset. It rewards discipline, awareness, consistency, and intentional money management. Every dollar must have a purpose.

This strategy also forces homeowners to rethink the relationship between debt and liquidity. Traditional financial advice sometimes encourages people to aggressively pay off debt while ignoring cash reserves. Although reducing debt is important, becoming completely illiquid can create vulnerabilities. A family that applies every extra dollar toward mortgage principal may later face emergencies that require expensive borrowing. Velocity banking attempts to maintain financial flexibility while simultaneously accelerating debt reduction.

Another important concept involves understanding average daily balance calculations. Many revolving accounts calculate interest based on daily balances rather than fixed monthly snapshots. This means even temporary reductions in balance may lower interest costs. When income is deposited earlier and debt balances remain lower for longer periods throughout the month, interest exposure decreases incrementally. Over time, these small improvements may create meaningful savings.

Velocity banking also highlights the importance of attacking principal directly rather than merely maintaining minimum payment structures. Standard mortgage payments are designed to maximize lender profitability over long periods. Extra principal reductions interrupt this structure and reduce future interest calculations. Even modest additional principal payments early in the loan term may save substantial amounts of money over the life of the mortgage. Some critics misunderstand velocity banking because they assume it depends entirely on borrowing against home equity irresponsibly. In reality, the strategy works best when borrowers already have positive monthly cash flow, stable income, and controlled spending habits. The objective is not to use debt recklessly but to reorganize financial systems more efficiently. Like any financial strategy, success depends on execution.

This chapter is not intended to suggest that everyone should immediately open a HELOC or restructure their entire financial life overnight. Instead, the goal is to build foundational understanding. Before implementing any advanced mortgage payoff strategy, homeowners must first understand how money flows through their financial system. Without this awareness, even powerful financial tools can become dangerous.

One of the hidden strengths of velocity banking is psychological momentum. Many homeowners become discouraged because traditional mortgages reduce principal very slowly in the beginning years. It can feel as though financial progress is invisible. Velocity banking often creates faster visible reductions in debt balances, which may increase motivation and reinforce disciplined financial behavior. Small victories compound psychologically just as interest compounds financially. Another critical factor is income stability. Individuals with predictable income patterns often find velocity banking easier to manage because they can forecast cash flow more accurately. Self-employed borrowers, commission earners, and business owners may still benefit significantly, but they must account for irregular income fluctuations carefully. Conservative planning becomes essential in these situations.

Emergency reserves also remain extremely important. One of the biggest mistakes borrowers make is attempting aggressive debt payoff without maintaining financial protection. Unexpected medical bills, job loss, business slowdowns, or major repairs can destabilize even well-designed financial systems. Velocity banking should complement financial stability, not replace it. Responsible planning always includes risk management.

As homeowners begin understanding these principles, they often realize that financial acceleration is less about earning extraordinary income and more about maximizing efficiency. Many high-income earners remain financially trapped because their expenses rise alongside their income. Meanwhile, disciplined households with moderate incomes sometimes achieve financial independence much faster because they control cash flow strategically. The philosophy behind velocity banking ultimately centers on intentionality. Instead of allowing banks, billing cycles, and default financial systems to dictate long-term outcomes, borrowers take a more active role in managing debt reduction. They begin understanding how interest behaves, how timing impacts balances, and how financial habits shape long-term wealth creation.

Over the coming chapters, you will learn how to structure these systems more specifically. You will explore practical applications, common mistakes, implementation strategies, and risk considerations. You will also discover that velocity banking is not merely a debt payoff tactic but a broader mindset focused on financial efficiency and acceleration.

The journey toward mortgage freedom does not begin with complicated spreadsheets or advanced financial products. It begins with understanding how money moves, how debt behaves, and how intentional financial systems can dramatically change long-term outcomes. Once this foundation becomes clear, the possibility of accelerating financial freedom becomes far more realistic.

The Family That Refused to Stay in Debt Forever

When Daniel and Sofia Ramirez bought their first home, they felt proud, relieved, and terrified all at the same time. After years of renting small apartments and moving between neighborhoods, they finally held the keys to a modest three-bedroom home in a quiet suburb outside Orlando. The house was not luxurious, but to them it represented stability, safety, and the beginning of a better future for their children.

The mortgage payment was larger than anything they had ever committed to financially. Daniel worked as a project manager for a construction company while Sofia operated a small home-based bookkeeping business. Together they earned enough to qualify for the loan comfortably, but the thirty-year mortgage still felt overwhelming. When Daniel looked at the amortization schedule for the first time, he nearly dropped the paperwork.

"How is this possible?" he asked one evening at the kitchen table. "We're going to pay almost double the price of the house over time."

Sofia stared quietly at the numbers. Month after month, most of the payment went toward interest while the principal balance barely moved.

“It feels like we’ll never own this place,” she said softly.

For the first year, they followed the standard routine. Paychecks came in. Bills went out. Mortgage payment drafted automatically each month. Whatever small amount remained was placed into savings or spent on unexpected expenses. Despite working hard, they felt financially stuck. Then one afternoon, Daniel overheard a conversation at work between two coworkers discussing mortgage payoff strategies. One of them mentioned something called velocity banking. Daniel had never heard the term before.

That night, curiosity pulled him into hours of research. He watched videos, read articles, studied financial examples, and filled notebooks with calculations. At first, the strategy sounded almost too simple. Use cash flow more efficiently. Reduce interest exposure. Attack principal strategically. Improve the movement of money instead of simply increasing income.

Still skeptical, Daniel spent weeks studying the concept before discussing it seriously with Sofia.

"I don't want us doing something risky," she warned.

"Neither do I," Daniel replied. "But I think we've been taught to think about money the wrong way."

Together they reviewed their finances carefully. They discovered something surprising. Although they were not wealthy, they consistently generated positive monthly cash flow. The problem was not necessarily income. The problem was inefficiency. Money flowed through their accounts without strategy.

They decided to begin conservatively. First, they built a stronger emergency reserve. Sofia insisted on this step before changing anything else financially. Once they had several months of reserves saved, they opened a modest home equity line of credit with a conservative limit. Daniel created spreadsheets tracking every dollar entering and leaving the household.

At first, the process felt strange. Their income deposits now flowed into the revolving account structure instead of sitting untouched in a traditional checking account. They monitored balances constantly. Every extra dollar was directed strategically.

The first few months required adjustment. Sofia became more intentional with grocery spending. Daniel reduced unnecessary subscription services and impulse purchases. They were not living miserably, but they became aware of financial leakage that previously went unnoticed.

Then something unexpected happened.

The mortgage balance began dropping faster than they had imagined.

For the first time since purchasing the house, they could visibly see progress. Instead of feeling trapped in a never-ending thirty-year cycle, they felt movement. Momentum. Control.

Daniel became obsessed with learning more about financial systems. He studied amortization schedules during lunch breaks. He analyzed how interest accumulated daily. He explored budgeting strategies and debt acceleration concepts. The more he learned, the more frustrated he became that basic financial education was rarely taught in schools.

Meanwhile, Sofia discovered another unexpected benefit. The strategy forced them to communicate better about money. Instead of avoiding financial discussions due to stress, they now reviewed goals together regularly. Their marriage improved because they began operating as a financial team rather than two individuals reacting emotionally to bills.

Over the next three years, their financial transformation accelerated.

Daniel received occasional performance bonuses at work, which they applied strategically toward principal reduction. Sofia expanded her bookkeeping business and increased her monthly income gradually. Instead of increasing lifestyle spending dramatically, they focused on strengthening cash flow.

Friends and relatives often questioned why they remained so disciplined.

"You need to enjoy life too," one friend joked after Daniel declined buying a luxury SUV.

Daniel smiled politely. "We are enjoying life. We're building freedom."

By year five, the results became undeniable. Their mortgage balance had fallen dramatically faster than projected under the original loan schedule. More importantly, they no longer felt financially suffocated. The reduction in interest expenses improved monthly flexibility. Stress levels declined. Confidence increased.

Then came the opportunity that changed everything.

A small rental property became available near Sofia's parents' neighborhood. It needed cosmetic repairs, but the price was reasonable. Years earlier, the idea of purchasing an investment property would have felt impossible. Now, because of improved equity position, disciplined cash flow management, and stronger financial confidence, they had options.

After careful planning, they purchased the property conservatively. Rental income covered the expenses while creating additional monthly cash flow. Instead of simply accelerating mortgage payoff, they had begun building wealth.

One evening, Daniel sat outside on the patio watching his children play in the backyard. Sofia joined him quietly.

"Remember when we thought we'd be trapped in debt forever?" she asked. Daniel laughed softly. "I remember feeling like the mortgage owned us."

"And now?"

He looked around at the house, the yard, and the life they had slowly built.

"Now I feel like we're finally taking ownership of our future."

Sofia smiled. "The crazy thing is we didn't become rich overnight."

"No," Daniel said. "We just became intentional."

Years later, their original mortgage was nearly gone. The rental property had appreciated significantly. Their savings had grown steadily. Most importantly, they had developed financial habits that changed the trajectory of their family permanently.

Their children grew up hearing conversations about budgeting, investing, debt management, and financial discipline. Money was no longer a source of fear inside the home. It became a tool, a system, and a pathway toward freedom.

Daniel often reflected on how small changes created massive long-term results. They had not discovered a magic shortcut. They had simply learned how money truly worked and refused to stay trapped inside systems designed to keep people paying interest forever.

The greatest lesson they learned was not about mortgages or lines of credit. It was about awareness. Once they understood how cash flow, debt, and interest interacted together, they could never look at money the same way again.

And that understanding changed their family's future forever.

Chapter 2

How Interest Really Works — Why Most Homeowners Stay in Debt for Decades

Most homeowners believe that if they consistently make their mortgage payment every month, they are making meaningful progress toward owning their home free and clear. While technically true, the reality is often far more discouraging. The structure of traditional mortgages is specifically designed to maximize long-term interest collection for lenders. Many borrowers spend years making payments without realizing how slowly their principal balance declines during the early stages of the loan. Understanding how interest truly works is one of the most important steps toward understanding why velocity banking can potentially accelerate debt payoff dramatically.

Interest is the price borrowers pay for access to money. When a bank lends money for a mortgage, it assumes risk and expects compensation for allowing the borrower to use those funds over time. The longer the repayment period, the more interest the lender earns. This is why thirty-year mortgages generate significantly more total interest than fifteen-year mortgages, even when the interest rate itself may be relatively similar. The majority of homeowners focus almost entirely on the monthly payment amount rather than the total cost of the loan. Banks understand this psychological behavior extremely well. A lower monthly payment often feels more comfortable, even if it results in paying substantially more interest over time. Stretching repayment over thirty years reduces the immediate monthly burden but increases long-term lender profitability enormously.

One of the most misunderstood concepts in mortgage lending is amortization. Amortization refers to the process of gradually repaying a loan through scheduled payments over time. Each mortgage payment contains two major components: principal and interest. In the beginning years of the loan, the majority of the payment goes toward interest rather than reducing the principal balance. Only later in the loan term does the principal reduction begin accelerating more significantly.

For example, a homeowner with a large mortgage may discover that after several years of payments, only a relatively small portion of the original balance has actually been eliminated. This often shocks borrowers because emotionally they feel they have been making substantial progress simply by paying consistently every month. In reality, the lender has collected a significant amount of interest during that same period.

This structure explains why making additional principal payments early in the loan term can create powerful long-term savings. Since future interest calculations depend on the remaining balance, reducing principal earlier decreases the amount of future interest charged over the life of the loan. Small principal reductions today may create disproportionately large savings decades later.

Many people mistakenly believe that all monthly payments are equal in financial impact. In reality, timing matters tremendously. A payment applied directly toward principal early in the loan may save far more money than the same payment applied later. This is because interest compounds over time. The earlier principal is reduced, the less interest continues accumulating moving forward.

Velocity banking builds upon this understanding by focusing aggressively on principal reduction and interest efficiency. Instead of passively accepting the standard amortization structure, the strategy attempts to interrupt it. The goal is not simply to make minimum required payments forever but to reduce balances strategically and accelerate the speed at which debt disappears.

Another important concept is daily interest accumulation. Many revolving credit products calculate interest based on average daily balances. This means balances fluctuating throughout the month can directly impact interest charges. Lower balances maintained for longer periods may reduce overall interest costs incrementally. Velocity banking often leverages this principle by directing income into revolving accounts strategically.

To fully understand why traditional debt structures keep people financially trapped for decades, homeowners must also recognize the emotional side of debt management. Most borrowers are conditioned to think short-term. They prioritize keeping monthly obligations manageable rather than minimizing total long-term cost. As a result, they often refinance repeatedly, extend loan terms, increase consumer debt, and delay financial freedom unknowingly.

Banks and lenders are not necessarily doing anything unethical. Their business model simply relies on long-term lending profitability. Mortgage products are structured mathematically to generate steady returns over extended periods. Borrowers who understand these structures can make more informed decisions about how to manage their debt more efficiently.

One major issue many households face is that they rarely calculate the true lifetime cost of borrowing. They focus on whether they can qualify for the payment rather than analyzing how much interest they will ultimately pay. This mindset often leads to financial complacency. People accept decades of debt as normal because they have never been taught to question the structure itself.

Another critical factor is lifestyle inflation. As income rises, many homeowners increase spending proportionally instead of accelerating debt reduction. Larger homes, luxury vehicles, vacations, subscriptions, and consumer financing often absorb additional earnings. Even high-income households can remain trapped financially when expenses continually rise alongside income. Understanding interest becomes meaningless if financial behavior remains undisciplined.

This chapter is not meant to create fear around mortgages. Real estate ownership remains one of the most powerful long-term wealth-building tools available when managed responsibly. Mortgages allow families to purchase homes, build equity, stabilize housing costs, and benefit from appreciation over time. The issue is not the existence of debt itself but rather the inefficient management of long-term interest accumulation.

Velocity banking attempts to shift the borrower's relationship with debt. Instead of accepting slow amortization passively, borrowers begin actively managing cash flow to reduce interest exposure. Every financial decision becomes more intentional. The borrower starts thinking strategically about where money sits, how balances fluctuate, and how timing affects long-term outcomes.

One powerful realization many people experience is understanding that interest works in both directions. When borrowers carry long-term debt inefficiently, compound interest benefits the lender. However, when borrowers reduce debt aggressively and free up cash flow earlier, they can redirect that money into investments, retirement accounts, businesses, or appreciating assets where compounding begins working in their favor instead.

The concept of financial acceleration becomes extremely important here. The faster debt disappears, the faster cash flow becomes available for wealth-building activities. A family that eliminates a large mortgage years earlier than scheduled may redirect thousands of dollars per month into investments for decades afterward. The long-term impact can become life-changing.

Another overlooked issue involves financial stress. Long-term debt obligations create emotional pressure that affects relationships, career decisions, and lifestyle flexibility. Many people remain trapped in jobs they dislike simply because large monthly obligations leave little room for risk or transition. Reducing debt faster can create emotional freedom alongside financial freedom. It is also important to recognize that not every debt payoff strategy works equally well for every household. Some homeowners benefit from conservative approaches. Others may prioritize investing over aggressive mortgage reduction depending on interest rates, investment opportunities, tax strategies, and personal goals. Velocity banking is one strategy among many, but understanding how interest functions remains universally valuable regardless of which path a person ultimately chooses.

Education changes perspective. Once homeowners truly understand amortization, daily interest calculations, and long-term borrowing costs, they begin viewing financial decisions differently. The mortgage payment stops feeling like an unavoidable life sentence and instead becomes a system that can potentially be optimized and accelerated through intentional planning.

One of the greatest financial shifts occurs when individuals stop thinking only in terms of payments and begin thinking in terms of balance reduction. Minimum payments maintain debt. Strategic principal reduction destroys debt. This distinction becomes foundational to everything that follows in velocity banking.

The chapters ahead will continue building upon these principles. You will learn how cash flow positioning, revolving credit tools, structured payment systems, and disciplined financial management can potentially shorten payoff timelines dramatically. But none of these strategies matter without first understanding the true nature of interest and why so many homeowners unknowingly remain trapped inside long-term debt structures for most of their adult lives.

Once you understand how the system works, you can begin building a strategy that works for you instead of simply working for the system.

The Mortgage That Controlled Everything

Marcus and Elena Foster believed they were successful.

They owned a beautiful home in a growing suburban neighborhood, drove newer vehicles, took occasional vacations, and earned a combined household income that placed them comfortably above average. From the outside, their lives appeared stable and impressive. Friends complimented their house constantly. Family members admired how far they had come financially.

But behind closed doors, Marcus felt trapped.

Every month seemed to revolve around bills. Mortgage payment. Car payments. Insurance. Credit cards. Utilities. School expenses for the kids. Medical bills. Subscriptions. Repairs. The money arrived quickly and disappeared even faster.

One evening, Marcus sat at the dining room table reviewing their finances while Elena folded laundry nearby.

"I don't understand how we make this much money and still feel broke," he muttered.

Elena sighed. "Because everything costs more now."

Marcus shook his head slowly. "No, it's more than that."

He opened the mortgage statement again. They had lived in the house for nearly six years. Thousands upon thousands of dollars had already been paid to the lender.

Yet the balance barely seemed lower.

"How is this possible?" he asked. "We've paid so much already."

Elena walked over quietly and stared at the statement beside him.

"That can't be right," she whispered.

Marcus had recently discovered the amortization schedule hidden deep within their original loan documents. Until then, neither of them fully understood how mortgage interest actually worked. Most of their payments during the early years had gone almost entirely toward interest.

The realization hit Marcus hard.

"We're not building freedom," he said quietly. "We're feeding debt."

That night changed something inside him.

Over the next several weeks, Marcus became obsessed with understanding how loans, interest, and debt structures really worked. He watched educational videos late into the night after the kids went to bed. He read books about financial systems. He studied mortgage amortization tables during lunch breaks at work.

The more he learned, the more frustrated he became.

Nobody had ever taught him this.

Not in school. Not in college. Not during the mortgage process. Nobody had explained how long-term interest quietly consumed wealth over decades.

One Saturday morning, Marcus spread papers across the kitchen counter. “I think we’ve been thinking about money completely wrong,” he told Elena. She raised an eyebrow cautiously. “What do you mean?”

“We focus on payments instead of ownership. We focus on affordability instead of total cost.”

Elena sat down slowly as Marcus showed her the numbers. Thirty years of payments. Hundreds of thousands in interest. The true cost of carrying long-term debt.

“It feels overwhelming,” she admitted.

Marcus nodded. “It is. Unless we change how we manage money.”

At first, Elena resisted his growing interest in advanced debt strategies. She worried he would become obsessed with extreme budgeting or risky financial schemes. But Marcus reassured her repeatedly.

“I’m not trying to gamble,” he explained. “I just want to stop giving away so much of our future to interest.”

They began tracking their spending carefully for the first time in their marriage.

The results shocked them.

Hundreds of dollars disappeared monthly into unnecessary expenses they barely noticed before. Dining out. Random online purchases. Subscription services. Impulse spending after stressful workdays. Small leaks everywhere.

Individually, none of the expenses seemed catastrophic. Combined, they represented enormous lost opportunity.

Marcus created spreadsheets showing how even modest additional principal payments could shorten the mortgage dramatically over time. Elena initially thought the calculations seemed exaggerated.

Then Marcus showed her something that changed her perspective completely.

"If we paid just a little extra consistently and controlled our cash flow better, we could save years of payments."

"Years?" she asked.

"Possibly more than a decade."

For the first time, the mortgage no longer felt permanent.

They started slowly. No drastic lifestyle changes. No unrealistic sacrifices. They simply became more intentional. Every financial decision now had a question attached to it:

Does this move us closer to freedom or further into debt?

That single question transformed their behavior. Marcus picked up occasional consulting projects outside his primary job. Elena expanded her online business carefully. Instead of automatically increasing lifestyle spending as income improved, they directed additional cash strategically toward debt reduction.

At first, progress felt small.

Then momentum began building.

After one year, the principal balance had dropped noticeably faster than before. The psychological impact was enormous. For the first time, they felt like they were winning instead of merely surviving.

One evening, Marcus looked at their updated loan projections and smiled.

"We're breaking the cycle," he said quietly.

Elena smiled back. "I finally feel hopeful."

As their financial understanding deepened, they became increasingly aware of how many people around them remained trapped in similar situations. Friends upgraded houses repeatedly while resetting thirty-year loan terms. Coworkers financed luxury lifestyles while carrying massive debt burdens. Families earned strong incomes yet remained financially fragile because cash flow constantly disappeared into interest obligations. Marcus no longer envied expensive lifestyles the way he once had.

He saw them differently now.

He saw the hidden cost behind the appearances.

Over the next several years, the Foster family transformed financially. Their emergency savings grew stronger. Consumer debt disappeared. Mortgage principal declined steadily. Financial stress inside the home decreased dramatically.

Perhaps most importantly, they gained flexibility.

Marcus eventually left the corporate position he disliked and started a smaller consulting business with greater schedule freedom. Elena spent more time with the children while continuing to grow her business part-time. Because debt obligations had decreased substantially, they no longer felt trapped by fear.

One afternoon, Marcus stood in the backyard watching his son practice soccer.

Years earlier, he would have been inside worrying about bills.

Now, for the first time in his adult life, he felt financially in control.

Not because he had become extraordinarily wealthy overnight.

But because he finally understood how money truly worked.

The mortgage had once controlled everything — their stress, their choices, their future, and their freedom.

Now, they were slowly taking control back.

And with every principal reduction, every strategic payment, and every intentional financial decision, the chains of long-term debt grew weaker.

For Marcus and Elena, understanding interest changed more than their mortgage.

It changed the direction of their entire lives.

Chapter 3

The Power of Cash Flow — Why Income Management Matters More Than Income Size

One of the greatest financial myths in modern society is the belief that higher income automatically creates wealth and financial freedom. While income certainly matters, countless high earners remain deeply trapped in debt, financial stress, and long-term obligations despite earning far more than the average household. At the same time, some individuals with moderate incomes steadily build wealth, eliminate debt early, and create long-term financial stability. The difference often comes down to one critical factor: cash flow management.

Velocity banking is built upon the principle that how money moves through your financial system matters more than simply how much money you earn. A household generating strong positive cash flow with disciplined financial habits may accelerate debt reduction far more effectively than a household earning twice as much but spending inefficiently. Understanding this concept is essential because velocity banking does not rely solely on increasing income. Instead, it focuses on maximizing the efficiency of existing cash flow.

Cash flow refers to the movement of money entering and leaving your financial life. Income flowing in through salaries, business revenue, commissions, investments, or rental income represents positive cash flow. Mortgage payments, debt obligations, utilities, insurance, groceries, taxes, and discretionary spending represent outgoing cash flow. The relationship between these inflows and outflows determines financial flexibility, debt acceleration potential, and long-term wealth-building capability.

Most people live reactively rather than strategically when it comes to cash flow. Income arrives, bills are paid, discretionary spending follows, and whatever remains is often minimal. Little attention is given to timing, efficiency, or intentional allocation. This passive approach keeps many households financially stagnant regardless of income level. Velocity banking challenges this behavior by treating cash flow as an active financial weapon rather than simply a monthly survival mechanism.

One of the key reasons cash flow matters so much is because debt acceleration depends on surplus financial capacity. If every dollar earned is immediately consumed by obligations and lifestyle expenses, there is little room to attack principal aggressively. Conversely, even modest positive cash flow, when managed strategically over long periods, can create powerful momentum toward debt elimination and wealth accumulation.

This chapter is not about extreme budgeting or living a miserable life. Financial acceleration does not require eliminating every enjoyable expense or sacrificing all comfort. Instead, it requires awareness. Many people lose substantial amounts of money through unconscious financial leakage. Small recurring expenses, impulse purchases, lifestyle inflation, and inefficient spending habits quietly consume enormous amounts of potential wealth over time.

For example, a household may increase spending automatically every time income rises. A raise at work leads to a more expensive vehicle. A successful business year leads to luxury upgrades. Higher earnings create larger obligations instead of greater freedom. This pattern traps many high-income earners in perpetual financial dependence despite strong salaries.

Velocity banking introduces a different philosophy. Instead of allowing lifestyle expansion to absorb every financial improvement, excess cash flow becomes a tool for reducing liabilities strategically. The faster debt declines, the faster monthly obligations decrease. As obligations shrink, additional cash flow becomes available, creating an accelerating cycle of financial improvement. One of the most powerful aspects of cash flow optimization is its compounding effect. Small monthly improvements may appear insignificant initially, but over years they create dramatic results. An extra few hundred dollars consistently directed toward principal reduction can shorten loan timelines substantially. When combined with reduced interest accumulation, these incremental improvements compound powerfully over time.

Many homeowners mistakenly believe they must wait until they earn substantially more money before improving their financial situation. While increased income certainly helps, financial discipline often matters first. Without disciplined cash flow management, additional income frequently disappears into larger expenses and lifestyle obligations. Learning how to control money effectively at current income levels creates the foundation for handling greater financial success responsibly later.

Velocity banking often works best for individuals who understand exactly where their money goes each month. This requires honest financial analysis. Many households underestimate discretionary spending significantly because expenses occur gradually and emotionally. Coffee purchases, dining out, streaming services, online shopping, convenience spending, and entertainment costs may seem minor individually but collectively reduce financial acceleration dramatically. Another critical component of cash flow management is timing. Money sitting idle in low-efficiency accounts while high-interest debt accumulates creates financial drag. Velocity banking attempts to reposition income strategically to reduce average debt balances and minimize unnecessary interest exposure. This concept becomes especially important when using revolving credit structures responsibly.

One reason many financially successful individuals focus heavily on cash flow rather than net worth alone is because cash flow creates flexibility. A person with significant assets but poor liquidity may still experience financial stress. Conversely, strong positive cash flow provides options, resilience, and financial breathing room. Velocity banking relies heavily on this principle because maintaining controlled liquidity while accelerating debt reduction often creates greater long-term stability.

Emergency preparedness also becomes essential in cash flow planning. Some people aggressively pursue debt payoff while neglecting reserves entirely. This creates vulnerability because unexpected expenses may force reliance on expensive consumer debt later. Strong financial systems balance debt acceleration with stability and protection. Velocity banking should increase financial control, not create fragility. Another important lesson involves understanding behavioral spending patterns. Financial decisions are often emotional rather than logical. Stress, insecurity, social pressure, boredom, and lifestyle comparison frequently drive unnecessary spending. Many individuals unconsciously spend money seeking temporary emotional satisfaction while sacrificing long-term freedom. Awareness of these habits becomes crucial for successful cash flow optimization.

The psychology of cash flow management also impacts motivation. Traditional mortgage structures often feel discouraging because progress appears painfully slow. Strategic cash flow systems, however, may create visible financial momentum more quickly. Watching balances decline faster can reinforce discipline and increase confidence. Momentum becomes psychologically powerful.

Income variability must also be addressed carefully. Self-employed individuals, business owners, real estate professionals, commission earners, and entrepreneurs often experience fluctuating income patterns. While velocity banking can still work effectively in these situations, conservative planning becomes extremely important. During strong income months, surplus cash flow may accelerate debt reduction significantly. During slower months, liquidity management becomes essential. Technology and automation can also improve cash flow awareness dramatically. Budget tracking systems, automated transfers, spending reports, and financial dashboards help households monitor behavior more effectively. The goal is not obsession but intentionality. Financial clarity reduces waste and improves decision-making.

Another overlooked factor is the opportunity cost of poor cash flow management. Every dollar lost unnecessarily to interest or lifestyle inflation represents money that cannot be invested elsewhere. Over decades, this opportunity cost becomes enormous. Funds redirected toward investments, businesses, retirement accounts, or appreciating assets may compound significantly over time once debt obligations decline.

Velocity banking ultimately teaches homeowners to view income differently. Instead of merely using income to survive month-to-month, income becomes a strategic resource designed to create acceleration. Every dollar gains purpose. Every financial decision carries long-term implications. Money begins working proactively instead of reactively.

One of the greatest transformations many people experience through structured cash flow management is emotional peace. Financial stress often comes not only from income limitations but from lack of control. When people begin understanding where their money goes and how to direct it intentionally, anxiety frequently decreases. Confidence grows because financial outcomes no longer feel random or uncontrollable. This chapter is not suggesting perfection is necessary. Every household makes mistakes, experiences setbacks, and faces unexpected challenges. The goal is progress, not perfection. Small improvements maintained consistently over long periods create life-changing results. Financial acceleration rarely happens overnight. Instead, it emerges gradually through disciplined systems and intentional behavior.

As you continue through this book, you will begin learning how to structure cash flow more specifically within the velocity banking framework. You will explore strategies involving revolving credit, principal reduction techniques, debt prioritization, and payment timing systems. However, none of those advanced strategies matter without first mastering the foundation of cash flow awareness.

Income matters. But how you manage income matters even more.

The homeowner who controls cash flow intelligently may ultimately achieve greater financial freedom than the high earner who allows money to flow carelessly through their life without structure or purpose. Understanding this principle changes everything about how debt, wealth, and financial independence are approached moving forward.

The Couple Who Made Six Figures but Felt Broke

Ryan and Melissa Carter earned more money than they ever imagined possible when they first got married.

Ryan worked in medical sales, earning commissions that fluctuated but often reached impressive levels during strong quarters. Melissa managed operations for a growing logistics company and earned a stable salary with annual bonuses. Together, their household income exceeded what most of their friends earned.

Yet despite the strong income, they constantly felt pressure.

Every month seemed tight.

Every unexpected expense created stress.

Every financial conversation turned tense.

Their home was beautiful. Their vehicles were expensive. Vacations looked impressive on social media. But privately, they felt trapped by obligations that seemed to expand endlessly.

One evening, Ryan walked into the kitchen carrying the mail.

"We got another credit card statement," he muttered. Melissa barely looked up from her laptop. "Just pay it."

Ryan tossed the envelope onto the counter. "That's the problem. We always just pay everything without understanding where the money keeps going."

Melissa sighed heavily. "We make good money, Ryan. We shouldn't have to stress this much."

But they did.

The mortgage payment consumed a huge portion of their income. Car payments added another layer of pressure. Dining out, subscriptions, luxury purchases, travel expenses, and random online shopping quietly drained thousands every month. Because their income remained strong, they rarely questioned the pattern deeply.

Until Ryan lost a major client.

Almost overnight, his commission income dropped sharply. Panic entered the household immediately.

Suddenly, the lifestyle they had built felt fragile.

Ryan spent sleepless nights staring at spreadsheets while Melissa tried reassuring him that things would recover soon.

But the fear exposed something deeper. They were financially dependent on maintaining extremely high income levels simply to support their existing obligations.

One Saturday morning, Ryan sat alone at the kitchen table reviewing bank statements from the previous six months. What he discovered shocked him.

Thousands of dollars had disappeared into expenses they barely remembered making.

Luxury dinners. Weekend shopping trips. Subscription services. Upgraded electronics. Convenience spending. Emotional spending after stressful workdays.

Individually, none of it seemed catastrophic.

Collectively, it was devastating.

When Melissa woke up, she found Ryan surrounded by papers and spreadsheets.

"We're leaking money everywhere," he said quietly.

Melissa sat beside him cautiously. "How bad is it?"

Ryan handed her the reports.

For the next two hours, they reviewed their financial habits honestly for the first time in years.

The truth hurt. Despite earning excellent income, they had almost no intentional cash flow management. Money simply flowed in and flowed out automatically. Higher earnings had created a larger lifestyle rather than greater freedom.

Melissa leaned back silently.

"We look successful," she whispered. "But financially, we're exhausted."

That conversation became a turning point.

Instead of trying to maintain appearances endlessly, they decided to rebuild their financial life intentionally. Not through extreme deprivation, but through awareness and structure.

The first step was tracking every dollar.

At first, the process felt uncomfortable. They realized how emotionally driven many purchases had become. Stress often triggered spending. Boredom triggered spending. Social comparison triggered spending.

Ryan canceled subscriptions they rarely used. Melissa started meal planning more carefully. They reduced unnecessary shopping habits. Instead of buying things automatically, they paused before spending.

"Does this actually improve our life?" became their new question. Surprisingly, many purchases failed the test.

Within several months, their cash flow improved dramatically without destroying their quality of life. For the first time in years, money remained available at the end of the month instead of disappearing instantly.

Ryan then discovered advanced mortgage acceleration concepts and became fascinated by cash flow strategy.

"What if we used our income more intentionally instead of just surviving month-to-month?" he asked Melissa one evening.

She smiled cautiously. "As long as we don't become weird finance robots."

Ryan laughed. "No promises."

Slowly, they began restructuring how money moved through their household. Extra cash flow started attacking debt instead of funding lifestyle upgrades. Their mortgage principal began declining faster. Credit card balances disappeared. Savings increased steadily.

The psychological impact surprised them most.

Stress inside the home decreased dramatically.

Money conversations no longer felt like arguments. Instead, they became planning sessions about goals, freedom, and long-term opportunities.

One evening, Melissa looked at their updated financial projections and shook her head in disbelief.

"We've earned good money for years," she said. "But this is the first time I actually feel financially stable."

Ryan nodded. "Because now the money has direction."

Over time, Ryan's commissions recovered and eventually surpassed previous levels. But something had changed permanently.

Instead of inflating their lifestyle again, they strengthened their financial systems further.

When friends upgraded homes, Ryan and Melissa stayed where they were. When coworkers purchased luxury vehicles, they kept their current cars longer. They no longer felt the same pressure to impress others financially.

Freedom mattered more now.

Several years later, their mortgage balance had dropped dramatically. Investments had grown steadily. Consumer debt was gone entirely. Their monthly obligations had decreased enough that Melissa eventually reduced her work hours to spend more time with family. One afternoon, Ryan sat outside watching their daughter ride her bicycle down the driveway.

Years earlier, he had believed financial success meant looking wealthy.

Now he understood something completely different.

True financial success was flexibility.

It was peace.

It was having options.

It was knowing that income no longer controlled every decision because cash flow was finally under control.

Melissa walked outside carrying coffee and sat beside him.

"Do you remember how stressed we used to be all the time?" she asked.

Ryan smiled softly. "We thought we needed more money."

"And really?"

"We needed a better system."

Their lives had not transformed because they suddenly became millionaires.

They transformed because they learned how to manage the money already flowing through their lives. And once they mastered cash flow, everything else began changing with it.

Chapter 4

Understanding HELOCs and Revolving Credit — The Core Tools Behind Velocity Banking

One of the most important concepts in velocity banking is understanding the difference between traditional installment debt and revolving credit. Most people spend their entire financial lives using installment loans without fully understanding how they work. Mortgages, auto loans, student loans, and personal loans all generally follow fixed repayment structures. Borrowers receive a lump sum upfront and repay the debt gradually over time through scheduled monthly payments. While this structure creates predictability, it also limits flexibility and often maximizes long-term interest paid to the lender.

Velocity banking introduces a different way of thinking by incorporating revolving credit tools, particularly home equity lines of credit, commonly known as HELOCs. These accounts function differently than traditional loans and may create opportunities for strategic debt acceleration when used responsibly. However, before implementing any strategy involving revolving credit, homeowners must understand exactly how these financial tools operate, including both their advantages and risks.

A HELOC is a revolving line of credit secured by the equity in your home. Equity represents the difference between your home's value and the remaining balance owed on your mortgage. For example, if your home is worth $500,000 and you owe $300,000 on your mortgage, you may have approximately $200,000 in equity before accounting for lender loan-to-value restrictions. A lender may allow you to borrow a portion of that equity through a HELOC.

Unlike a traditional mortgage where funds are distributed one time only, a HELOC allows repeated access to funds during the draw period. Borrowers may borrow, repay, and reuse the line of credit multiple times, similar to how a credit card functions. Interest is typically charged only on the outstanding balance rather than the total approved limit. This flexibility is one of the reasons HELOCs play a central role in many velocity banking strategies.

The concept behind velocity banking is not simply borrowing more money. In fact, the goal is usually the opposite: reducing total debt faster and more efficiently. The HELOC becomes a cash flow management tool that allows borrowers to position income strategically to reduce interest exposure and accelerate principal reduction.

One of the most important mechanics behind HELOCs is average daily balance interest calculation. Many revolving accounts calculate interest daily based on the outstanding balance. This means the timing of deposits and withdrawals directly impacts how much interest accumulates over time. When balances remain lower throughout the month, interest costs may decrease incrementally.

For example, if a borrower deposits their paycheck directly into a HELOC account, the balance immediately decreases, reducing interest exposure. As bills and expenses are paid throughout the month, the balance gradually increases again. However, because the balance remained lower for part of the month, less interest may accumulate compared to leaving the money sitting idle in a traditional checking account.

At first glance, these reductions may appear small. However, over months and years, the compounding effect may become significant. Velocity banking focuses heavily on these cumulative efficiencies.

Another important characteristic of HELOCs is payment flexibility. During the draw period, borrowers often have flexible repayment options. Some lenders require only interest payments, while others allow larger principal reductions voluntarily. This flexibility can be beneficial for disciplined borrowers who want to accelerate debt reduction strategically.

However, flexibility also creates risk.

Many people misuse revolving credit because they treat available credit as extra income instead of temporary leverage. They repeatedly borrow against equity without reducing overall debt balances long-term. This behavior often leads to deeper financial problems rather than greater freedom. Because HELOCs are secured by the home itself, irresponsible borrowing may place the property at risk.

That is why velocity banking requires discipline, organization, and consistent positive cash flow. The strategy does not work effectively for individuals who overspend impulsively or rely heavily on debt to maintain lifestyle expenses. A HELOC should never become a tool for financing luxury purchases, vacations, or uncontrolled spending habits.

Another important consideration involves variable interest rates. Many HELOCs carry adjustable rates tied to broader market interest conditions. As rates rise, borrowing costs may increase substantially. Borrowers implementing velocity banking strategies must plan conservatively and ensure they could still manage payments under less favorable rate environments. This is why strong emergency reserves remain essential. Financial systems should never depend entirely on perfect economic conditions. Unexpected events such as job loss, medical emergencies, business slowdowns, or rising interest rates may place pressure on household finances. Velocity banking should improve financial control, not create fragility.

Loan structure also matters tremendously. Most HELOCs include two major phases: the draw period and the repayment period. During the draw period, borrowers may access and repay funds flexibly. Once the repayment period begins, access to additional borrowing ends and required repayment structures often become more aggressive. Homeowners must understand these timelines before implementing long-term strategies.

One of the most popular techniques within velocity banking is known as chunking. Chunking involves using available revolving credit strategically to make large lump-sum reductions toward mortgage principal. After the chunk payment is made, future income and cash flow are directed aggressively toward paying down the HELOC balance. Once the HELOC balance decreases sufficiently, another chunk payment may be applied to the mortgage. The reason chunking can potentially create significant savings is because large principal reductions early in the mortgage term interrupt amortization aggressively. Since future mortgage interest calculations depend on the remaining balance, reducing principal earlier may dramatically reduce long-term interest accumulation.

However, chunking requires careful planning. Borrowers must fully understand their monthly cash flow and ensure they can comfortably replenish the HELOC balance without financial strain. Aggressive chunking without proper budgeting may create instability quickly.

Another benefit of HELOC-based strategies is liquidity management. Traditional mortgage overpayments become trapped inside home equity unless refinanced or borrowed against later. A HELOC maintains greater flexibility because available credit may become accessible again after repayment. This can provide financial breathing room during emergencies when managed responsibly.

Still, easy access to credit can also become psychologically dangerous. Some individuals feel tempted to spend simply because funds are available. This is why emotional discipline remains one of the most important components of successful velocity banking. Financial tools amplify behavior. Responsible behavior creates acceleration. Undisciplined behavior creates risk. Credit scores also influence HELOC effectiveness significantly. Borrowers with strong credit profiles generally qualify for lower interest rates and better terms. Improving credit before applying for a HELOC may therefore improve long-term results substantially.

Homeowners should also evaluate lender fees, annual charges, closing costs, prepayment penalties, and promotional rate structures carefully. Some HELOC products advertise attractive introductory terms that later adjust upward significantly. Understanding the complete loan structure is essential before committing to any strategy.

Another major misconception is that HELOCs automatically create wealth. They do not. A HELOC simply creates flexibility. Whether that flexibility becomes beneficial or harmful depends entirely on how the borrower uses it. Used strategically, revolving credit may accelerate debt reduction and improve financial efficiency. Used irresponsibly, it may increase debt and financial stress.

Velocity banking therefore requires a mindset shift. Instead of viewing money passively, borrowers begin actively managing cash flow, interest exposure, and liquidity positioning. Every dollar gains strategic importance. Income stops merely covering expenses and begins serving a broader purpose of financial acceleration. This chapter is not intended to encourage reckless borrowing or unrealistic expectations. The purpose is education. Understanding how revolving credit functions allows homeowners to evaluate whether these tools align with their personal financial goals, discipline level, income stability, and risk tolerance.

Financial freedom rarely comes from one single tactic. Instead, it emerges through consistent intentional decisions over time. HELOCs and revolving credit may become powerful components within that process when paired with discipline, education, and structured planning.

As you continue through this book, you will learn how these concepts connect with payment timing, cash flow cycling, debt prioritization, and long-term wealth creation. But none of those advanced strategies matter unless you first understand the foundation behind the tools themselves.

Knowledge creates control.

And control creates financial acceleration.

How Velocity Banking with a HELOC May Accelerate Mortgage Payoff

Let's walk through a simplified real-world example to understand how a HELOC and cash flow strategy may potentially reduce mortgage interest and accelerate payoff.

Scenario:

Home Value: $500,000 Current Mortgage Balance: $350,000 Mortgage Interest Rate: 6.5% fixed Remaining Mortgage Term: 30 years Monthly Mortgage Payment (Principal & Interest): Approximately $2,212

Household Monthly Net Income: $8,000 Monthly Living Expenses (excluding mortgage): $4,500 Positive Monthly Cash Flow: $1,288

Available HELOC Limit: $80,000 HELOC Starting Balance: $0 HELOC Interest Rate: 8%

Under a traditional mortgage structure, the borrower simply makes the required monthly payment of $2,212 every month for 30 years.

Total Paid Over 30 Years:

$2212 \times 360 = 796{,}320$

Total Mortgage Cost = Approximately $796,320

Total Interest Paid:

$796{,}320 - 350{,}000 = 446{,}320$

Total Interest = Approximately $446,320

Now let's look at a simplified velocity banking scenario.

Step 1: Use HELOC for a Chunk Payment

The borrower pulls $40,000 from the HELOC and immediately applies it toward the mortgage principal.

New Mortgage Balance:

350,000−40,000=310,000

This large principal reduction immediately lowers future mortgage interest accumulation because the mortgage balance is now smaller.

Step 2: Redirect Cash Flow Toward HELOC Paydown

The borrower now aggressively pays down the HELOC using monthly positive cash flow.

Monthly Positive Cash Flow Available:

8,000−4,500−2,212=1,288

The borrower applies approximately $1,288 monthly toward the HELOC balance.

In addition, all paychecks are deposited into the HELOC first, temporarily reducing average daily balances and reducing interest exposure throughout the month.

Approximate Time to Repay HELOC Chunk:

$40{,}000 \div 1{,}288 \approx 31$

Approximately 31 months, not including additional savings from reduced average daily interest exposure or bonuses/tax refunds.

Step 3: Repeat the Process

Once the HELOC balance decreases substantially, another chunk payment may be applied toward the mortgage.

Each chunk payment reduces mortgage principal earlier in the amortization schedule, potentially saving large amounts of future interest.

Example of Interest Savings Potential

If the borrower reduces the effective mortgage term from 30 years to approximately 18 years through aggressive chunking and disciplined cash flow management, total interest may decrease dramatically.

Approximate Total Paid Over 18 Years:

$2212 \times 216 = 477{,}792$

Approximate Interest Paid:

477,792−350,000=127,792

Approximate Interest Savings Compared to Original Loan:

446,320−127,792=318,528

Potential Interest Savings = Approximately $318,528

Important Reality Check

This example is simplified for educational purposes only. Real-world results vary based on:

- HELOC interest rates
- Mortgage rates
- Income consistency
- Spending discipline
- Additional lump sums
- Emergencies or financial setbacks
- Variable interest rate adjustments
- Taxes and fees
- Timing of deposits and payments

Velocity banking is not magic. The strategy works primarily because of:

1. Faster principal reduction
2. Improved cash flow efficiency
3. Reduced long-term mortgage interest exposure
4. Financial discipline and consistency

The borrower does not eliminate debt overnight. Instead, they strategically reposition cash flow to accelerate debt destruction while reducing wasted interest over time.

When implemented responsibly, the combination of cash flow management, HELOC flexibility, and disciplined principal reduction may potentially shorten mortgage timelines dramatically and free up future cash flow for investing, retirement, business ownership, or long-term wealth building.

Chapter 5

The Chunking Strategy — Using Strategic Lump-Sum Payments to Destroy Mortgage Principal Faster

One of the most powerful concepts within velocity banking is the strategy commonly referred to as "chunking." While the term may sound simple, the underlying financial impact can be significant when implemented correctly. Chunking focuses on making large, targeted reductions toward mortgage principal using available cash flow and revolving credit tools strategically. Instead of relying solely on standard monthly payments, borrowers interrupt the mortgage amortization schedule aggressively by applying substantial lump-sum payments directly toward principal balances.

To understand why chunking can potentially create dramatic long-term savings, homeowners must first understand how traditional mortgages behave over time. Most mortgages are heavily front-loaded with interest. During the early years of repayment, a large percentage of each monthly payment goes toward interest rather than principal reduction. This structure benefits lenders because interest accumulates most heavily when balances remain large. The faster principal decreases, however, the less future interest can accumulate. This is the foundation behind chunking. Large principal reductions early in the loan term may save substantial amounts of future interest because the lender no longer calculates interest on the higher original balance moving forward.

Traditional monthly mortgage payments reduce debt slowly because they follow a fixed amortization structure. Chunking attempts to disrupt this structure by introducing larger reductions periodically. These lump-sum reductions may come from bonuses, business income, side income, tax refunds, investment profits, disciplined savings, or strategically managed revolving credit such as a HELOC.

One of the key principles of chunking is timing. A large principal reduction made early in the mortgage term generally creates far more long-term savings than the same amount applied later. This happens because future interest calculations compound over time. Every dollar removed from principal today eliminates years of future interest accumulation attached to that dollar.

For example, applying a $25,000 lump sum toward a mortgage balance during year two of a loan may potentially save far more total interest than applying the same amount during year twenty. The earlier principal disappears, the earlier future interest calculations shrink.

Velocity banking often combines chunking with cash flow cycling. Borrowers may temporarily use revolving credit strategically to create larger principal reductions, then aggressively replenish the revolving balance through future income and positive monthly cash flow. This process may then repeat multiple times throughout the life of the loan.

However, chunking is not simply about moving debt around. The strategy only works effectively when overall debt decreases steadily over time. If borrowers continue increasing spending or fail to replenish revolving balances responsibly, the strategy collapses. Discipline remains absolutely essential.

One of the psychological advantages of chunking is visible progress. Traditional mortgage repayment often feels discouraging because balances decline slowly during the early years. Homeowners may make payments faithfully for years without feeling substantial progress emotionally. Chunking creates larger visible balance reductions, which often increases motivation and reinforces disciplined behavior.

Another major benefit of chunking involves cash flow liberation. As mortgage balances decline faster, future interest obligations shrink. Over time, this may create opportunities to redirect future cash flow toward investments, retirement accounts, businesses, emergency reserves, or additional real estate opportunities. Mortgage payoff acceleration therefore becomes part of a broader wealth-building strategy rather than merely a debt reduction exercise.

Many homeowners mistakenly assume they need extremely high incomes to benefit from chunking. While larger incomes certainly create greater flexibility, even moderate lump sums applied consistently over time may create meaningful long-term impact. The key is consistency and intentionality rather than perfection.

For example, annual tax refunds, work bonuses, commission spikes, side business income, or temporary reductions in expenses may all become opportunities for strategic chunk payments. Instead of allowing extra income to disappear into lifestyle inflation, chunking redirects temporary financial surpluses toward long-term financial acceleration.

One of the greatest threats to successful chunking is emotional spending. Many individuals experience increased income temporarily and immediately increase consumption rather than strengthening their financial position. Large bonuses often disappear into luxury purchases, vacations, vehicles, or impulse spending. Velocity banking encourages borrowers to view temporary financial surpluses strategically instead of emotionally.

Another important concept is understanding the difference between liquidity and trapped equity. Traditional extra mortgage payments become embedded inside home equity permanently unless refinanced or borrowed against later. Some homeowners worry that aggressive principal reductions may reduce liquidity access. This is one reason why velocity banking often incorporates revolving credit structures such as HELOCs, which may preserve flexibility while still accelerating debt reduction.

Still, maintaining balance remains critical. Over-aggressive chunking without adequate emergency reserves may create financial instability during unexpected situations. Responsible planning always includes emergency savings, conservative budgeting, and awareness of income stability.

Chunking strategies also work best when borrowers fully understand their monthly cash flow. If a household lacks positive cash flow consistently, aggressive chunking may create unnecessary pressure. The strategy works most effectively when supported by disciplined budgeting and stable income management.

Another overlooked advantage of chunking is the reduction of financial stress over time. Many homeowners feel trapped emotionally by long-term mortgage obligations. Large balance reductions may create psychological momentum and optimism. The realization that debt freedom could arrive years earlier than expected often transforms how people view money, work, and long-term planning.

However, chunking is not a get-rich-quick strategy. Mortgage acceleration still requires patience, discipline, and consistency. Some online presentations exaggerate results unrealistically, promising complete mortgage elimination within impossibly short timeframes regardless of income or financial situation. Responsible implementation requires realism.

Interest rates also influence chunking effectiveness. Higher mortgage rates generally increase the value of accelerated principal reduction because future interest savings become larger. Lower mortgage rates may shift some strategic priorities toward investing depending on long-term financial goals, investment returns, tax considerations, and risk tolerance.

Another major factor is opportunity cost. Every dollar directed toward mortgage reduction cannot simultaneously be invested elsewhere. This creates important strategic decisions. Some individuals prioritize debt freedom emotionally and psychologically. Others prioritize maximizing long-term investment growth. Velocity banking often attempts to create a middle ground by improving cash flow efficiency while reducing long-term debt faster.

Chunking may also create significant long-term compounding advantages beyond mortgage savings alone. Once debt obligations decrease substantially, freed cash flow may be redirected toward appreciating assets. The earlier mortgage debt disappears, the earlier investment compounding may accelerate in the borrower's favor instead of primarily benefiting the lender.

One important lesson homeowners eventually learn is that large financial transformations often result from repeated small strategic actions rather than one dramatic event. Consistent chunk payments applied over years may shorten mortgage terms dramatically without requiring unrealistic sacrifices. Financial acceleration emerges gradually through disciplined systems and intentional behavior.

Technology can also improve chunking effectiveness. Mortgage calculators, amortization software, budgeting systems, and financial tracking tools allow borrowers to model various payoff scenarios and understand the long-term impact of strategic payments more clearly. Seeing projected interest savings visually often strengthens motivation significantly.

Communication between spouses or partners also becomes extremely important when implementing chunking strategies. Financial acceleration works best when all household decision-makers understand the plan clearly and support the long-term goals involved. Misalignment creates tension, confusion, and inconsistent behavior.

One of the most empowering aspects of chunking is that it changes the homeowner's relationship with debt psychologically. Instead of feeling passively trapped inside a thirty-year repayment structure, borrowers begin actively controlling the pace of their financial future. Debt stops feeling permanent and begins feeling manageable, measurable, and conquerable.

Ultimately, chunking is not about financial perfection. It is about financial intentionality. Every strategic principal reduction weakens future interest accumulation. Every disciplined cash flow decision strengthens long-term freedom. Every avoided lifestyle inflation trap accelerates future flexibility.

The purpose of chunking is not merely to eliminate a mortgage faster. The deeper purpose is reclaiming control over cash flow, reducing dependency on long-term debt, and creating opportunities for greater financial independence moving forward. When understood and implemented responsibly, chunking becomes one of the most powerful tools within the broader velocity banking framework.

How Chunking May Potentially Save Hundreds of Thousands in Mortgage Interest

Scenario:

Original Mortgage Balance: $450,000 Mortgage Interest Rate: 7% fixed Original Loan Term: 30 years Monthly Principal & Interest Payment: Approximately $2,994

Total Cost Under Traditional 30-Year Mortgage:

$2994 \times 360 = 1{,}077{,}840$

Total Paid Over 30 Years = Approximately $1,077,840

Total Interest Paid:

$1{,}077{,}840 - 450{,}000 = 627{,}840$

Total Interest = Approximately $627,840

Now let's introduce a chunking strategy.

The homeowner receives:

- Annual work bonus: $15,000

- Tax refund annually: $5,000
- Side business income savings annually: $10,000

Total Annual Chunk Payment Available:

15,000+5,000+10,000=30,000

The borrower decides to apply a $30,000 chunk payment toward the mortgage principal every year in addition to making the regular mortgage payment.

Year 1 Example

Original Mortgage Balance:

450,000

After First Annual Chunk Payment:

450,000−30,000=420,000

Now future mortgage interest calculations are based on a significantly lower balance much earlier in the loan term.

Projected Payoff Impact

Instead of taking 30 years to repay the mortgage, consistent annual chunk payments of $30,000 may potentially reduce the payoff timeline to approximately 12–14 years depending on payment timing and amortization structure.

Approximate Total Paid Over 14 Years:

Regular Mortgage Payments for 14 Years:

$2994 \times 168 = 502{,}992$

Total Chunk Payments Over 14 Years:

$30{,}000 \times 14 = 420{,}000$

Approximate Total Paid:

$502{,}992 + 420{,}000 = 922{,}992$

Approximate Interest Paid:

$922{,}992 - 450{,}000 = 472{,}992$

Estimated Interest Savings:

$627{,}840 - 472{,}992 = 154{,}848$

Estimated Interest Savings = Approximately $154,848

Now let's combine chunking with improved monthly cash flow management.

Additional Monthly Principal Payment Suppose the borrower also improves budgeting and frees up an additional $1,000 per month to apply directly toward mortgage principal.

Additional Annual Principal Reduction:

$1{,}000 \times 12 = 12{,}000$

Combined Annual Extra Principal:

$30{,}000 + 12{,}000 = 42{,}000$

Potential Payoff Timeline:

The mortgage may potentially be eliminated in approximately 9–11 years depending on interest calculations and payment timing.

Potential Total Interest Savings:

$627{,}840 - 300{,}000 \approx 327{,}840$

Potential Interest Savings = Approximately $327,840

Psychological Impact Example

Original Mortgage Timeline:

30 years = 360 monthly payments

Accelerated Chunking Timeline:

10 years = 120 monthly payments

Payments Eliminated:

$360-120=240$

The borrower potentially eliminates 240 future mortgage payments.

Cash Flow Freedom After Mortgage Payoff

Once the mortgage disappears, the homeowner may redirect the former mortgage payment toward investing.

Former Mortgage Payment:

$2994\times12=35{,}928$

Annual Cash Flow Freed = Approximately $35,928

If invested annually at an average 8% return for 20 years:

Approximate Future Value = Over $1.6 million

Final Lesson

The true power of chunking is not simply paying off a mortgage faster.

The real power is:

- Reducing long-term interest exposure
- Accelerating principal reduction
- Freeing future cash flow earlier
- Redirecting money toward wealth-building assets
- Creating financial flexibility and freedom years sooner

Small strategic actions repeated consistently over time may completely transform long-term financial outcomes.

Chapter 6

The Role of Discipline and Financial Behavior — Why Velocity Banking Fails for Some People

One of the biggest misconceptions surrounding velocity banking is the belief that the strategy itself guarantees financial success. In reality, no financial strategy works independently of human behavior. Velocity banking is not magic, nor is it a shortcut that automatically eliminates debt regardless of spending habits, emotional discipline, or financial decision-making. The true success or failure of velocity banking depends less on mathematical formulas and more on personal behavior, consistency, and self-control.

Many people become excited when they first learn about accelerated mortgage payoff strategies. They see examples of reduced interest costs, shortened loan terms, and increased cash flow freedom. However, some individuals attempt to implement these systems without first addressing the financial habits that created long-term debt problems in the first place. As a result, they misuse revolving credit, overspend emotionally, and ultimately create larger financial problems rather than financial freedom. Velocity banking amplifies financial behavior. For disciplined individuals, it may accelerate debt reduction and wealth building. For undisciplined individuals, it may accelerate financial instability. Understanding this truth is critical before implementing any advanced mortgage payoff system.

One of the most dangerous financial behaviors is confusing available credit with available income. When borrowers open a HELOC or access revolving credit, the available balance may create a false sense of financial security. Some people begin using credit for vacations, luxury purchases, dining, entertainment, or lifestyle upgrades instead of strategic debt reduction. This behavior destroys the entire purpose of velocity banking.

A HELOC is not additional income. It is borrowed money secured by the home itself. Every dollar used irresponsibly increases financial risk. The homeowner's property becomes exposed to unnecessary leverage. That is why financial discipline must come before financial strategy.

Another common problem involves emotional spending. Many people use money psychologically rather than strategically. Stress, anxiety, insecurity, boredom, social comparison, and temporary emotional highs frequently drive purchasing decisions. Retail therapy, impulse buying, lifestyle upgrades, and convenience spending often occur unconsciously. Velocity banking requires awareness strong enough to interrupt these patterns consistently.

For example, some homeowners receive bonuses or extra income and immediately increase spending rather than strengthening their financial position. New vehicles, vacations, electronics, designer products, and lifestyle inflation absorb cash flow that could have accelerated debt reduction dramatically. The issue is rarely income alone. The issue is behavior attached to income.

One of the most powerful concepts in financial acceleration is delayed gratification. Velocity banking often requires temporarily sacrificing short-term pleasures to create long-term freedom. This does not mean living miserably or eliminating all enjoyment from life. Instead, it means learning how to prioritize future flexibility over temporary emotional satisfaction.

Discipline also matters because velocity banking requires consistency. A single large principal payment may create temporary progress, but long-term acceleration occurs through repeated intentional actions maintained over years. Sporadic financial enthusiasm followed by uncontrolled spending usually produces disappointing results. Sustainable systems matter more than temporary motivation.

Budgeting therefore becomes a foundational component of successful velocity banking. Many people dislike the word "budget" because they associate it with restriction or punishment. In reality, budgeting simply means giving money direction intentionally. Without a clear understanding of where money goes each month, it becomes impossible to optimize cash flow effectively.

One of the most important habits homeowners can develop is tracking expenses honestly. Many households dramatically underestimate discretionary spending because expenses occur gradually. Daily coffee purchases, food delivery, subscriptions, online shopping, entertainment costs, convenience spending, and small impulse purchases may appear harmless individually but collectively drain enormous amounts of financial potential over time.

Another behavioral issue involves lifestyle inflation. As income rises, many people automatically increase expenses proportionally. A raise at work leads to a more expensive vehicle. A successful business year leads to a larger home. Higher earnings trigger higher obligations instead of greater financial freedom. This pattern traps many high-income earners in perpetual debt cycles despite impressive salaries.

Velocity banking encourages the opposite mindset. Instead of immediately expanding lifestyle with every income increase, surplus cash flow may be directed toward debt acceleration, investing, or wealth-building assets. This creates financial leverage over time rather than long-term dependency on high income levels.

Communication between spouses or financial partners also plays an enormous role in success. Many households struggle financially not because of insufficient income but because of inconsistent financial philosophies. One partner may prioritize long-term goals while the other spends impulsively. One may value debt reduction while the other prioritizes appearances or lifestyle expansion. Without alignment, financial systems often break down.

Successful velocity banking households usually share several behavioral traits. They communicate openly about money. They track progress consistently. They avoid emotional financial decisions. They maintain emergency reserves. They live below their means. Most importantly, they understand that financial freedom is built gradually rather than instantly.

Another major factor is patience. Modern society promotes instant gratification constantly. People want immediate results, immediate upgrades, and immediate financial transformation. Velocity banking still requires time, discipline, and repetition. While the strategy may accelerate payoff timelines substantially, meaningful financial transformation still emerges over years of intentional behavior.

Fear and overconfidence can also both create problems.

Some individuals become too fearful to implement any strategy despite having strong financial stability and discipline. Others become overly aggressive and overleverage themselves recklessly. The healthiest approach typically involves balanced conservatism. Borrowers should understand risks clearly while implementing strategies responsibly and gradually.

Emergency reserves are another behavioral indicator of financial maturity. Many people aggressively pursue debt payoff while neglecting savings entirely. Then when unexpected expenses arise, they return to consumer debt immediately. Velocity banking should strengthen financial stability, not eliminate safety margins. Responsible borrowers maintain reserves alongside debt acceleration efforts.

Income stability also influences behavior significantly. Self-employed individuals, entrepreneurs, commission earners, and business owners often experience fluctuating cash flow. During strong income periods, confidence may rise excessively, leading to aggressive spending or overleveraging. Conservative planning during high-income periods helps stabilize long-term results.

Another overlooked aspect of financial discipline is resisting social pressure. Many households overspend attempting to match the lifestyles of friends, coworkers, relatives, or social media influencers. Expensive cars, luxury vacations, oversized homes, and status purchases often create hidden financial stress. Velocity banking requires enough confidence to prioritize long-term freedom over short-term appearances.

One of the greatest psychological transformations occurs when individuals stop using money primarily for validation. Instead of spending to impress others, they begin using money strategically to build flexibility, options, and peace of mind. Financial independence becomes more important than maintaining appearances.

This chapter is not intended to shame anyone for past mistakes. Nearly everyone has experienced periods of poor financial behavior, emotional spending, or financial confusion. The purpose is awareness. Once people understand the relationship between behavior and financial outcomes, they gain the ability to change patterns intentionally moving forward.

Another important lesson is that perfection is unnecessary. Financial acceleration does not require flawless execution forever. Setbacks, emergencies, mistakes, and unexpected expenses are part of real life. The goal is progress and consistency over time rather than unrealistic perfection.

Technology may also support behavioral improvement. Expense tracking apps, automated savings systems, budgeting software, and financial dashboards increase awareness and reduce unconscious spending patterns. Automation often improves consistency by reducing emotional decision-making.

One of the greatest benefits of disciplined financial systems is reduced stress. Financial chaos creates anxiety because outcomes feel unpredictable and uncontrollable. Structured cash flow management, strategic debt reduction, and intentional spending create emotional stability alongside financial improvement.

Velocity banking ultimately teaches that financial freedom is less about mathematical complexity and more about behavioral consistency. Many people already earn enough money to improve their financial situation significantly. The challenge is learning how to manage that money intentionally rather than emotionally.

The tools themselves are neutral. HELOCs, revolving credit,

chunking strategies, and accelerated payment systems can either create freedom or increase risk depending on behavior. Financial tools simply magnify habits already present.

That is why the true foundation of velocity banking is not revolving credit.

It is discipline.

Without discipline, even the best strategy may fail.

With discipline, even moderate income households may transform their financial future dramatically over time.

How Financial Behavior Impacts Velocity Banking Results

Scenario 1 — Disciplined Borrower

Mortgage Balance: $400,000 Mortgage Interest Rate: 6.75% Monthly Mortgage Payment: Approximately $2,594

Monthly Household Net Income: $9,000 Monthly Expenses (excluding mortgage): $4,500

Positive Monthly Cash Flow:

9,000−4,500−2,594=1,906

The disciplined borrower uses a HELOC strategically and applies the entire $1,906 positive cash flow monthly toward debt reduction.

Additional Annual Bonus Applied to Principal:

10,000

Total Additional Principal Reduction Per Year:

Monthly Extra Principal:

$1{,}906 \times 12 = 22{,}872$

Total Including Bonus:

$22{,}872 + 10{,}000 = 32{,}872$

Estimated Result:

Instead of taking 30 years to repay the mortgage, the disciplined borrower may potentially eliminate the mortgage in approximately 13–15 years depending on payment timing and HELOC structure.

Potential Interest Savings:

Original 30-Year Interest Estimate:

$2{,}594 \times 360 = 933{,}840$

Total Original Interest:

933,840−400,000=533,840

Estimated Accelerated Interest Paid:

300,000

Potential Interest Savings:

533,840−300,000=233,840

Potential Savings = Approximately $233,840

Scenario 2 — Undisciplined Borrower

Same Mortgage: $400,000 Same Income: $9,000 monthly Same HELOC Structure

However, this borrower increases lifestyle spending.

Additional Monthly Expenses:

- Dining out: $600
- Vehicle upgrade: $500
- Online shopping: $400
- Vacation financing: $300

Additional Lifestyle Inflation:

600+500+400+300=1,800

New Monthly Expenses:

4,500+1,800=6,300

Remaining Monthly Cash Flow:

9,000−6,300−2,594=106

The borrower now has almost no positive cash flow available for debt acceleration.

Worse, suppose the borrower also uses the HELOC for lifestyle purchases:

Vacation Charged to HELOC:

15,000

Furniture Purchase:

8,000

Vehicle Down Payment:

12,000

Total Non-Strategic HELOC Usage:

15,000+8,000+12,000=35,000

Instead of reducing debt, the borrower increases total liabilities.

Estimated Result:

- Mortgage payoff remains close to original 30 years
- Additional HELOC interest accumulates
- Financial stress increases
- Cash flow flexibility disappears
- Risk exposure rises dramatically

Behavior Difference

Disciplined Borrower:

- Uses HELOC strategically
- Maintains positive cash flow
- Reduces debt consistently
- Avoids lifestyle inflation
- Builds long-term financial flexibility

Undisciplined Borrower:

- Treats HELOC as extra income
- Increases spending emotionally
- Maintains high debt balances
- Sacrifices long-term freedom for short-term gratification

Final Lesson

The math behind velocity banking matters.

But behavior matters even more.

Two households with identical incomes, identical mortgages, and identical HELOC structures may experience completely different outcomes depending entirely on discipline, spending habits, and long-term financial behavior.

The strategy itself is only a tool.

Financial freedom ultimately comes from the habits of the person using it.

Chapter 7

Building the Velocity Banking System — Step-by-Step Implementation for Real Life

Understanding the concepts behind velocity banking is important, but knowledge alone does not create financial acceleration. The true transformation begins when homeowners learn how to apply these principles systematically in real life. Many people become excited after learning about mortgage payoff acceleration, HELOC strategies, and chunking techniques, yet they never create a structured implementation plan. Without organization, discipline, and step-by-step execution, even the best financial strategies often fail.

Velocity banking works best when approached as a complete financial system rather than a random collection of isolated tactics. The goal is not simply making occasional extra payments. The objective is creating an intentional structure where cash flow, debt reduction, liquidity management, and spending behavior all work together toward long-term financial freedom.

One of the first steps in building a successful velocity banking system is conducting a complete financial inventory. Many homeowners attempt advanced strategies without fully understanding their current financial position. Before implementing any revolving credit or chunking strategy, borrowers should know exactly how much income they earn, where their money goes each month, what debts they carry, what interest rates they pay, and how much positive monthly cash flow exists consistently.

This process often becomes eye-opening. Many households discover they spend far more than they realized on discretionary expenses, subscriptions, convenience spending, or lifestyle inflation. Others discover that despite strong incomes, very little surplus cash flow remains available for acceleration because obligations have expanded excessively over time. Honest awareness is the foundation of successful implementation.

The second major step involves establishing financial stability before acceleration. Velocity banking should never be built on financial chaos. Homeowners should prioritize stabilizing overdue accounts, reducing high-interest consumer debt where appropriate, building emergency reserves, and organizing monthly cash flow before aggressively implementing advanced strategies. Emergency savings remain extremely important. One of the biggest mistakes people make is pursuing aggressive mortgage payoff while leaving themselves financially vulnerable. Unexpected medical bills, job loss, business slowdowns, or home repairs may quickly force borrowers back into expensive debt if reserves are inadequate. A stable financial foundation creates resilience.

Once stability is established, homeowners can begin evaluating whether a HELOC or revolving credit structure fits their situation appropriately. Not every borrower needs a HELOC, and not every homeowner qualifies for favorable terms. Strong credit profiles, stable income, positive equity, and disciplined financial habits generally improve suitability for these strategies.

Choosing the right HELOC also matters significantly. Borrowers should compare lenders carefully, evaluating interest rates, variable rate structures, closing costs, annual fees, draw periods, repayment terms, and overall flexibility. Some HELOCs appear attractive initially but later become expensive due to rising rates or hidden fees. Education and caution remain essential.

After establishing the revolving credit structure, the next step is reorganizing cash flow intentionally. Traditional banking systems typically separate checking accounts, savings accounts, and debt payments without strategic interaction. Velocity banking restructures this flow to maximize interest efficiency.

In many implementations, income deposits are directed into the revolving account first. This temporarily lowers the outstanding balance and reduces average daily interest exposure. As monthly expenses are paid throughout the month, the balance rises gradually again. The objective is keeping balances lower for longer periods whenever possible.

At the same time, disciplined budgeting becomes critical. Every dollar must have purpose. Velocity banking rewards intentional spending patterns because excess cash flow drives acceleration. The larger the consistent positive monthly cash flow, the faster the debt reduction process may occur.

One of the most important implementation concepts is identifying the first chunk payment opportunity. This may come from available HELOC funds, savings beyond emergency reserves, bonuses, commissions, side business income, tax refunds, or other financial surpluses. The borrower applies a strategic lump sum directly toward mortgage principal to interrupt amortization aggressively.

The psychological effect of the first chunk payment is often powerful. Homeowners who previously felt trapped in slow mortgage repayment suddenly witness meaningful balance reduction. This visible progress often strengthens commitment to the overall strategy. After the chunk payment occurs, the system enters the replenishment phase. During this phase, positive monthly cash flow is directed aggressively toward reducing the HELOC balance. Once the revolving balance decreases sufficiently, another chunk payment may be applied strategically. Over time, this cycle repeats repeatedly.

However, successful implementation requires patience. Many people expect unrealistic overnight results after seeing exaggerated online examples. Real-world velocity banking still takes years of consistent discipline. The strategy accelerates financial freedom gradually rather than instantly.

Another critical implementation principle involves maintaining spending control during financial improvement. As mortgage balances decline and cash flow improves, some individuals become overconfident and begin increasing lifestyle spending prematurely. This behavior weakens acceleration dramatically. Velocity banking works best when improved cash flow continues strengthening financial position rather than fueling unnecessary consumption.

Technology can significantly improve implementation consistency. Mortgage calculators, budgeting software, automatic payment systems, expense trackers, and financial dashboards help borrowers monitor progress clearly. Seeing declining balances visually often increases motivation substantially.

Tracking progress monthly also becomes important psychologically. Homeowners should monitor mortgage balance reductions, HELOC balance trends, interest savings estimates, and overall net worth growth over time. Progress tracking reinforces discipline and keeps long-term goals visible during slower periods.

Another major component of implementation involves flexibility. Financial life is never perfectly predictable. Unexpected expenses, income fluctuations, emergencies, and economic changes occur regularly. Velocity banking systems should adapt conservatively when circumstances change rather than forcing aggressive acceleration at all costs.

For example, during periods of economic uncertainty or unstable income, borrowers may temporarily prioritize liquidity and reserves over aggressive chunking. Conservative flexibility often creates stronger long-term outcomes than rigid overaggression.

Couples implementing velocity banking should also schedule regular financial reviews together. Miscommunication creates many financial problems inside households. Monthly reviews allow both partners to evaluate progress, discuss upcoming expenses, adjust priorities, and maintain alignment toward long-term goals.

One of the greatest benefits of systemized velocity banking is increasing financial awareness. Many homeowners operate financially on autopilot for years. Bills are paid mechanically without deeper understanding of how cash flow, interest, and debt interact. Velocity banking forces intentional engagement with financial behavior, which often creates broader improvements far beyond mortgage payoff alone.

Another important implementation lesson is understanding that velocity banking exists within a larger financial strategy. Mortgage acceleration should align with retirement planning, investment goals, tax considerations, business opportunities, family priorities, and long-term wealth creation objectives. The mortgage is only one piece of the overall financial picture.

For some individuals, maximizing investment growth may take priority over aggressive mortgage payoff depending on interest rates and expected investment returns. Others may prioritize emotional peace and debt freedom. Velocity banking should complement personal goals rather than override them blindly.

Risk management also remains central throughout implementation. Homeowners should avoid overleveraging themselves excessively, especially during volatile economic periods. Conservative chunk sizes, strong emergency reserves, manageable monthly obligations, and realistic expectations create healthier long-term results.

As implementation progresses successfully, many borrowers experience increasing momentum. Mortgage balances decline faster. Interest expenses shrink. Cash flow improves. Financial stress decreases. Confidence grows. Eventually, the system begins reinforcing itself psychologically because visible progress strengthens disciplined behavior.

One of the most empowering aspects of velocity banking is that it transforms the homeowner's role from passive borrower to active financial strategist. Instead of simply accepting a thirty-year repayment structure, borrowers begin intentionally controlling the speed of their financial future.

The system does not eliminate the need for work, discipline, or patience. But it creates the possibility of accelerating freedom dramatically compared to passive long-term debt management.

Ultimately, successful implementation depends on combining education, organization, discipline, and consistency. Financial freedom is rarely created through one dramatic event. Instead, it emerges through thousands of intentional financial decisions repeated steadily over time.

Velocity banking simply provides a framework for making those decisions more efficiently.

Step-by-Step Velocity Banking Implementation Example

This example shows a homeowner using a more advanced debt payoff strategy with a home and a HELOC (home equity line of credit). The home is worth $600,000, with a $420,000 mortgage at 6.75% interest. The monthly mortgage payment is $2,724. After all expenses, the household has strong positive cash flow of about $3,076 per month, and they also have access to a $100,000 HELOC they can use like a flexible credit tool.

The homeowner starts by using $50,000 from the HELOC and applies it directly to the mortgage. This reduces the mortgage balance from $420,000 to $370,000. The key idea is that lowering the mortgage balance immediately reduces how much interest builds up over time, which helps the homeowner save money long-term.

Next, every month the homeowner uses their $3,076 positive cash flow to pay down the HELOC. This means they are constantly "recycling" money between the mortgage and the HELOC. In about 12 to 16 months, the $50,000 HELOC balance is paid back, especially when extra income like a $15,000 yearly bonus is added. Once the HELOC is paid back, the homeowner repeats the process by taking another chunk (for example $40,000) and applying it to the mortgage again. This lowers the mortgage balance even more, from $370,000 down to $330,000. Over time, they keep repeating this cycle of using the HELOC, paying it down with income, and reducing the mortgage in chunks.

Instead of paying off the mortgage slowly over 30 years with a total cost of about $980,640 and $560,640 in interest, this strategy can potentially reduce the payoff time to around 13 years. In that case, total payments might drop to about $544,944, meaning interest paid could fall to about $124,944.

The key lesson is that when used responsibly, cash flow and tools like a HELOC can help speed up mortgage payoff dramatically. By using income, bonuses, and structured "chunk payments," homeowners may reduce interest costs, shorten debt timelines, and increase financial flexibility much faster than a traditional payment plan.

Chapter 8

The Risks of Velocity Banking — What Every Homeowner Must Understand Before Starting

Velocity banking has the potential to accelerate mortgage payoff, reduce long-term interest costs, and improve cash flow efficiency when implemented responsibly. However, one of the biggest mistakes homeowners make is focusing only on the potential rewards while ignoring the risks. Every financial strategy carries trade-offs, limitations, and potential dangers. The more flexible a financial tool becomes, the more discipline and responsibility are required to use it properly.

This chapter is critically important because many people discover velocity banking through overly simplified online presentations that emphasize dramatic mortgage payoff results without adequately discussing the risks involved. Some presentations make it sound as though anyone can eliminate decades of mortgage debt quickly regardless of income level, financial habits, or economic conditions. This creates unrealistic expectations and may encourage dangerous financial behavior.

Velocity banking is not appropriate for everyone.

Understanding who should avoid the strategy, what can go wrong, and how to reduce risk responsibly is essential before implementing any revolving credit or chunking system.

One of the biggest risks involves overspending. Because velocity banking often incorporates revolving credit such as a HELOC, borrowers gain access to large amounts of available credit. For disciplined individuals, this flexibility may improve financial efficiency. For undisciplined individuals, it may become extremely dangerous.

Many homeowners psychologically treat available credit as available money. Once a large HELOC becomes accessible, temptation increases. Some individuals begin using the line of credit for vacations, vehicles, furniture, luxury purchases, or emotional spending. Instead of reducing debt, they increase liabilities while believing they are following a financial strategy. This behavior often leads to financial instability rather than freedom.

Another major risk involves variable interest rates. Most HELOCs carry adjustable interest rates tied to broader market conditions. During periods of rising interest rates, monthly interest costs may increase significantly. Borrowers who initially felt comfortable with the strategy may suddenly experience cash flow pressure if rates rise aggressively. For example, a HELOC balance carrying a 5% interest rate may feel manageable initially. But if rates rise to 9% or higher, the financial math changes dramatically. Homeowners implementing velocity banking must stress-test their finances conservatively and ensure they could still manage balances comfortably under less favorable conditions.

Income instability also creates substantial risk.

Velocity banking works best for households with consistent positive cash flow. Borrowers who experience highly unpredictable income, unstable employment, or business volatility may struggle to replenish revolving balances effectively during slower periods. Without stable cash flow, aggressive chunking strategies may become dangerous quickly.

For self-employed individuals, commission earners, entrepreneurs, and business owners, conservative planning becomes especially important. During strong income periods, optimism may encourage overly aggressive financial decisions. However, business cycles and economic downturns can create sudden cash flow disruptions unexpectedly.

Emergency preparedness therefore becomes essential.

One of the worst mistakes homeowners make is eliminating liquidity entirely while pursuing accelerated debt payoff. If all available resources become tied up in home equity and an emergency occurs, borrowers may face serious financial pressure. Medical bills, home repairs, job loss, lawsuits, economic recessions, or family emergencies may force reliance on expensive debt or asset liquidation if reserves are insufficient.

Velocity banking should improve financial flexibility, not eliminate it.

Another overlooked risk involves behavioral fatigue. Some individuals begin velocity banking with strong enthusiasm but lose consistency over time. Budgeting discipline weakens. Spending increases gradually. Tracking systems become neglected. Eventually, the strategy deteriorates because behavioral consistency disappears.

Financial acceleration requires long-term discipline, not temporary motivation.

Many homeowners underestimate how emotionally difficult financial discipline can become over several years. Social pressure, lifestyle comparison, burnout, and unexpected life changes may weaken commitment gradually if the system is not realistic and sustainable. Relationship stress may also emerge if financial partners are not aligned completely. One spouse may prioritize aggressive debt reduction while the other values lifestyle flexibility or spending freedom more heavily. Without clear communication and shared goals, financial tension may increase significantly.

Another major risk involves overleveraging home equity. Some homeowners become overconfident after initial success and begin borrowing excessively against appreciating home values. This may create vulnerability during housing market downturns. If property values decline while leverage remains high, financial flexibility may disappear rapidly.

Real estate markets do not always rise continuously.

Economic recessions, housing corrections, rising interest rates, and local market disruptions may reduce property values unexpectedly. Borrowers relying heavily on home equity should maintain conservative loan-to-value ratios whenever possible.

There is also refinancing risk.

Some velocity banking strategies assume future refinancing opportunities or favorable lending conditions. However, economic environments change. Credit standards tighten during recessions. Property values fluctuate. Personal credit situations may change unexpectedly. Homeowners should never build financial systems that rely entirely on future refinancing assumptions. Another critical issue is misunderstanding the math itself.

Some people believe velocity banking creates savings merely because money moves differently between accounts. In reality, the strategy only works when debt balances decrease consistently and interest exposure declines meaningfully over time. Simply transferring balances between accounts without disciplined cash flow improvement creates no real financial advantage.

The true power of velocity banking comes from:

- Faster principal reduction
- Lower long-term interest accumulation
- Positive cash flow management
- Disciplined financial behavior
- Strategic timing of payments

Without these factors, the strategy becomes ineffective.

Tax implications may also matter depending on jurisdiction, loan structure, and how funds are used. Homeowners should consult qualified tax professionals before implementing large-scale financial restructuring strategies involving home equity or investment activities.

Psychological risk also deserves attention.

Some people become obsessed with debt elimination to unhealthy levels. They sacrifice all enjoyment, relationships, family experiences, or personal well-being purely to accelerate payoff timelines. Financial freedom should improve life, not create emotional exhaustion or extreme deprivation.

Balance matters.

The goal is intentionality, not financial obsession.

Another overlooked risk is opportunity cost. Every dollar directed toward accelerated mortgage reduction cannot simultaneously be invested elsewhere. In some situations, long-term investment opportunities may potentially outperform mortgage interest savings depending on interest rates, market returns, tax treatment, and risk tolerance. This does not make mortgage payoff wrong — it simply means financial decisions must align with broader goals thoughtfully.

Velocity banking is therefore not a universal solution.

Some individuals may benefit more from traditional investing strategies, retirement account maximization, business reinvestment, or conservative debt management approaches depending on their personal situation. The strategy should serve the individual's goals rather than become an emotional ideology.

One of the healthiest approaches is gradual implementation.

Instead of immediately applying extremely aggressive chunking strategies, many homeowners benefit from testing smaller systems first. Conservative experimentation allows borrowers to evaluate behavior, stress levels, cash flow consistency, and financial comfort before expanding the strategy further.

Monitoring results regularly also reduces risk substantially. Homeowners should review balances, interest costs, spending behavior, liquidity levels, and overall financial stability consistently. Problems caught early are usually manageable. Problems ignored for long periods often become much larger.

Another important lesson is understanding that financial strategies must evolve over time. A system that works well during one stage of life may require adjustment later. Marriage changes, children, business shifts, economic conditions, retirement planning, health concerns, and market environments all influence financial priorities.

Flexibility and awareness are therefore essential.

One of the greatest strengths of velocity banking, when implemented properly, is increased intentionality. Borrowers become more aware of how interest behaves, how money moves, and how financial decisions impact long-term outcomes. Even individuals who ultimately choose different strategies often benefit tremendously from the financial education gained through studying velocity banking principles.

Ultimately, risk is not something to fear blindly. Risk simply requires understanding and management.

Every financial decision involves trade-offs.

Keeping a thirty-year mortgage for decades carries risks. Aggressively paying down debt carries risks. Investing heavily carries risks. Starting businesses carries risks. The goal is not eliminating all risk entirely. The goal is choosing risks intentionally and responsibly based on personal goals, discipline, and financial capacity.

Velocity banking may become a powerful financial acceleration strategy for disciplined households with stable cash flow, strong budgeting habits, and conservative planning. But it requires maturity, patience, emotional control, and realistic expectations.

Understanding the risks clearly is not negative.

It is what allows the strategy to be implemented intelligently and safely.

How Velocity Banking Can Become Risky Without Proper Planning

In this example, we compare two borrowers using a HELOC strategy very differently. In Scenario 1, the homeowner is financially disciplined. They have a $500,000 mortgage at 6.25% interest with a monthly payment of about $3,078. Their household income is $14,000 per month, and after expenses and the mortgage, they still have strong positive cash flow of $4,422 each month. They also have $50,000 in emergency savings, which gives them a safety cushion.

This responsible borrower only uses $40,000 of their $150,000 HELOC limit to make a mortgage "chunk" payment. This reduces the mortgage balance to $460,000 immediately. Then, instead of overspending, they use their $4,422 monthly cash flow to pay back the HELOC. In about 9 months, the $40,000 is fully repaid. This strategy allows them to reduce debt while still staying financially safe, with savings and stability intact.

In Scenario 2, the borrower has the same income and mortgage but makes poor financial decisions by increasing lifestyle spending. They add luxury car payments, vacations, entertainment, shopping, and renovations, increasing monthly expenses by $4,500. This pushes their total expenses to $11,000 per month, leaving almost no money left after paying the mortgage. Because of this, their cash flow becomes negative, meaning they spend more than they earn. Even though they aggressively use the HELOC—taking out $160,000 total for mortgage payoff, vacations, cars, and home upgrades—they no longer have income left to properly repay it. This creates growing debt instead of financial progress.

The situation becomes even worse when interest rates rise. The HELOC balance becomes much more expensive to carry, and annual interest increases by thousands of dollars. On top of that, if income drops by $3,000 per month due to job changes or an economic slowdown, the borrower's monthly cash flow becomes deeply negative, making repayment even harder.

The key lesson is that the HELOC strategy itself is not good or bad—it depends entirely on behavior. The responsible borrower uses it carefully, keeps strong cash flow, and stays disciplined, which helps reduce debt safely. The overleveraged borrower, however, uses debt to fund lifestyle spending, loses cash flow control, and quickly falls into financial stress. The real difference between success and failure is not the tool—it is discipline, planning, and financial behavior.

Chapter 9

Combining Velocity Banking with Investing — Building Wealth While Accelerating Debt Payoff

One of the most important financial questions homeowners eventually face is whether they should focus primarily on paying off debt or investing for long-term wealth creation. Some financial experts strongly encourage eliminating all debt as quickly as possible. Others argue that investing aggressively while maintaining low-interest debt may create greater long-term financial growth. Velocity banking introduces an interesting middle ground by attempting to accelerate debt reduction while simultaneously improving future investing capacity and cash flow flexibility.

This chapter explores how velocity banking may potentially work alongside investing strategies rather than competing against them entirely. The goal is not merely eliminating a mortgage faster. The larger objective is improving long-term financial positioning so that future cash flow may eventually be redirected toward appreciating assets, retirement accounts, businesses, real estate portfolios, or other wealth-building opportunities. One of the biggest mistakes many homeowners make is viewing mortgage payoff and investing as completely separate financial goals. In reality, they are deeply connected because debt obligations directly impact cash flow. The faster major liabilities decline, the sooner income becomes available for investment and wealth accumulation.

Traditional thirty-year mortgages often delay serious investing opportunities because large monthly payments continue consuming cash flow for decades. Many families postpone investing aggressively, business ownership, or real estate expansion because debt obligations leave limited financial flexibility. Velocity banking attempts to shorten this timeline by reducing long-term interest exposure and accelerating debt reduction strategically.

However, understanding opportunity cost becomes extremely important.

Every dollar directed toward mortgage principal cannot simultaneously be invested elsewhere. Therefore, homeowners must evaluate interest rates, investment opportunities, risk tolerance, liquidity needs, tax considerations, and personal goals carefully when balancing debt acceleration with investing.

For example, suppose a homeowner carries a mortgage interest rate of 3%. If long-term investments are expected to generate significantly higher average returns over time, some individuals may prefer investing excess cash rather than aggressively paying down low-cost debt. On the other hand, if mortgage rates are much higher, accelerated payoff may create stronger guaranteed savings through reduced interest exposure.

Velocity banking often becomes especially attractive during higher interest rate environments because mortgage interest savings become more substantial. Reducing a 7% mortgage balance aggressively may create a strong risk-adjusted return through interest avoidance alone.

Another important concept is cash flow liberation. Once mortgage obligations disappear or decrease substantially, large amounts of monthly cash flow become available for investing automatically. This creates what many financially successful individuals refer to as financial acceleration. Debt reduction increases future investment capacity dramatically.

For example, eliminating a $3,000 monthly mortgage payment creates:

$3{,}000 \times 12 = 36{,}000$

Annual Cash Flow Freedom = $36,000

If that annual cash flow is redirected into long-term investments consistently, wealth accumulation may accelerate significantly over time.

Another major advantage of combining velocity banking with investing is psychological balance. Some individuals become extremely uncomfortable carrying debt and prioritize emotional peace over maximizing theoretical investment returns. Others feel anxious focusing solely on debt reduction while neglecting investment growth opportunities. Combining both approaches strategically may create a healthier emotional and financial balance.

Velocity banking also improves investing potential by reducing long-term interest drag. Interest paid to lenders represents money unavailable for investment compounding. Every dollar saved through reduced interest costs potentially becomes a future investment dollar instead. Over decades, this shift may create enormous differences in net worth.

Many homeowners underestimate how powerful investment compounding becomes once debt obligations shrink. Even moderate monthly investments maintained consistently over long periods may create substantial wealth due to compound growth.

For example, investing:

2,500×12=30,000 per year at an average 8% annual return over 20 years may potentially grow into several million dollars depending on market performance and contribution consistency.

One of the most effective long-term strategies often involves stages.

During early stages, homeowners may focus heavily on stabilizing finances, reducing high-interest debt, building emergency reserves, and accelerating mortgage payoff strategically. Once debt obligations decline substantially, future cash flow may shift increasingly toward investments and appreciating assets.

This staged approach creates flexibility because financial priorities naturally evolve throughout life.

Younger families may prioritize debt reduction and stability first. Later, investment growth and passive income creation may become larger priorities. Velocity banking can potentially shorten the timeline between these phases significantly.

Another important factor is risk tolerance.

Mortgage payoff creates guaranteed interest savings. Investments, however, involve uncertainty. Stock markets fluctuate. Real estate markets experience cycles. Businesses may fail. Some homeowners value the certainty of debt elimination more heavily than uncertain future investment returns. Others prioritize long-term growth potential despite short-term volatility.

Neither approach is universally correct.

Financial strategies must align with personal psychology, long-term goals, and emotional comfort levels.

Liquidity also matters.

Aggressively paying down a mortgage may reduce accessible cash reserves if too much capital becomes trapped inside home equity. Investments often provide greater liquidity depending on asset type. Velocity banking attempts to balance debt reduction with liquidity preservation through revolving credit structures and cash flow management.

However, overreliance on leverage creates risk. Some individuals become overly aggressive trying to simultaneously maximize investments and debt acceleration. Conservative balance remains important. Strong emergency reserves and manageable obligations should always remain priorities.

Another major benefit of combining investing with velocity banking is increased financial resilience. Multiple income streams and appreciating assets reduce dependence on employment income alone. Rental properties, retirement accounts, dividend investments, businesses, or passive income streams may eventually provide additional financial flexibility and security.

Many wealthy individuals focus heavily on cash flow rather than net worth alone. Velocity banking supports this philosophy because debt reduction increases future free cash flow available for asset accumulation.

Tax considerations may also influence strategic decisions. Mortgage interest, investment gains, retirement contributions, depreciation, and real estate income all carry varying tax implications depending on jurisdiction and personal financial structure. Consulting qualified financial and tax professionals may therefore become important for higher-income households implementing advanced strategies.

One overlooked advantage of debt acceleration is improved investment flexibility later. Individuals carrying large long-term debt obligations often feel unable to pursue entrepreneurial opportunities, career changes, real estate investing, or semi-retirement because monthly obligations remain too high. Reduced debt creates optionality.

Optionality is one of the most valuable forms of financial freedom.

It allows individuals to make decisions based on opportunity rather than fear.

Velocity banking also changes how people view income. Instead of merely using income to survive month-to-month, homeowners begin directing income strategically toward long-term wealth creation. Once this mindset develops, investing often becomes a natural extension of the broader financial acceleration system.

Another critical lesson involves avoiding extremes. Some individuals become obsessed with paying off every debt immediately while neglecting retirement savings entirely. Others invest aggressively while maintaining dangerous debt levels and minimal liquidity. Balanced strategies usually create stronger long-term outcomes than extreme approaches.

The most effective systems are sustainable emotionally and financially.

This chapter is not suggesting that every homeowner should aggressively invest while implementing velocity banking simultaneously. Instead, the purpose is understanding how debt reduction and investing interact together over time. Mortgage acceleration should support broader wealth creation goals, not exist independently from them. One of the greatest long-term advantages of accelerated mortgage payoff is time.

The earlier major debt disappears, the longer future cash flow may compound through investments instead of interest payments. Time magnifies financial decisions dramatically.

For example, someone who eliminates a mortgage ten years earlier may gain an additional decade of investment contributions and compound growth. That difference alone may potentially create hundreds of thousands or even millions of dollars in long-term net worth depending on contribution size and investment performance.

Ultimately, velocity banking is not merely about debt elimination.

It is about financial acceleration.

The true goal is creating flexibility, optionality, cash flow control, and long-term wealth-building capacity. Mortgage payoff simply becomes one important step within a much larger financial freedom journey.

When implemented responsibly, velocity banking may help homeowners shorten debt timelines while simultaneously creating future investing power far earlier than traditional mortgage structures typically allow.

How Accelerated Mortgage Payoff May Increase Long-Term Investment Wealth

In this example, a homeowner has a $450,000 mortgage at 6.5% interest with a monthly payment of about $2,844. If they follow a normal 30-year plan, they will end up paying about $1,023,840 total over the life of the loan, including about $573,840 in interest. This shows how expensive long-term mortgage interest can be when the loan is carried for the full 30 years.

We then compare two different strategies. Homeowner A follows the traditional approach by just making normal payments and waiting the full 30 years to finish the mortgage. They only start investing seriously after the house is fully paid off, which delays their ability to build wealth through investments.

Homeowner B uses an accelerated "velocity banking" style strategy. They add an extra $1,500 per month toward the mortgage and also apply a $12,000 annual bonus. This allows them to pay off the mortgage in about 15 years instead of 30, and they also save a large amount of interest over time.

Because they pay off the mortgage early, Homeowner B frees up their entire $2,844 monthly payment after year 15. They then invest that money for the next 15 years. Assuming an average 8% return, those investments can grow to over $925,000 by the end of the period. They also invest additional savings from reduced interest costs, adding another $270,000 or more in potential growth.

When you combine the accelerated mortgage payoff with investment growth, Homeowner B could potentially create over $1.5 million in total financial benefit compared to the traditional approach. This includes both interest savings and investment growth. Homeowner A, in contrast, builds wealth more slowly because they delay investing until after the mortgage is fully paid.

The key lesson is that paying off debt faster does more than just remove a payment—it can unlock years of extra investing time. When done with discipline and planning, accelerating a mortgage can free up cash flow earlier and give money more time to grow, which can significantly increase long-term wealth.

Chapter 10

The Ultimate Velocity Banking Blueprint — Integrating Everything into a Complete Financial System

At this point in the series, you have explored the core foundations of velocity banking, including how interest works, how cash flow affects debt acceleration, how revolving credit can be used strategically, how behavioral discipline determines outcomes, and how investing can be integrated into a broader wealth-building strategy. The final step is understanding how all of these pieces come together into a complete, real-world financial system that homeowners can actually implement consistently over time.

The ultimate goal of velocity banking is not simply to pay off a mortgage faster. The deeper objective is to create a structured financial ecosystem where every dollar has a defined purpose, every financial decision is intentional, and every cash flow movement contributes either to debt reduction or wealth creation. When properly implemented, this system transforms a household from passive participants in long-term debt structures into active managers of financial acceleration. Most people approach their finances in a fragmented way. One account is used for income deposits. Another is used for bills. A separate savings account exists but is rarely optimized. Credit cards are used inconsistently. Debt payments are made automatically without strategic coordination. Investments, if they exist, are often disconnected from daily cash flow decisions. This fragmented approach creates inefficiency, wasted interest, and slow financial progress.

Velocity banking corrects this fragmentation by integrating all financial elements into one coordinated system. Income, expenses, debt, credit lines, and surplus cash flow all work together in a structured cycle. Instead of money flowing randomly through accounts, it follows a controlled path designed to reduce interest exposure and accelerate principal reduction.

The foundation of the system begins with cash flow awareness. Without understanding exactly how much money enters and leaves the household each month, no advanced strategy can function effectively. This is why financial tracking is not optional. It is the starting point. Every dollar must be accounted for so that inefficiencies can be identified and optimized.

Once cash flow is understood clearly, the next step is structuring liquidity. This typically involves maintaining emergency reserves to protect against unexpected events. Many households fail financially not because they lack income, but because they lack liquidity during emergencies. A strong financial system always prioritizes stability before acceleration.

After liquidity is established, revolving credit tools such as HELOCs may be introduced carefully. These tools are not required for every implementation, but they often serve as the central mechanism for cash flow cycling. The key is not maximizing credit usage, but optimizing timing and balance management to reduce interest exposure while maintaining flexibility.

The third layer of the system involves chunking strategy execution. This is where strategic lump-sum payments are applied to mortgage principal to interrupt amortization and reduce long-term interest accumulation. These chunk payments may come from bonuses, disciplined savings, side income, or structured cash flow cycles using revolving credit.

However, chunking alone is not enough. Without replenishment discipline, the system collapses. That is why every chunk payment must be followed by a structured replenishment phase, where positive monthly cash flow is directed toward restoring liquidity and reducing revolving balances. The fourth layer involves optimizing monthly cash flow efficiency. This means minimizing unnecessary spending, eliminating waste, and ensuring that surplus income is consistently directed toward financial acceleration. Small improvements in monthly cash flow may appear insignificant, but over time they create exponential effects when combined with interest reduction.

The fifth layer integrates long-term investing strategy. Once debt levels decrease and cash flow increases, surplus capital can be redirected into appreciating assets. This creates a dual acceleration effect where debt decreases while wealth accumulation increases simultaneously. The earlier debt is reduced, the earlier investing compounding can begin working at full strength.

One of the most important aspects of the ultimate blueprint is balance. Many people fail because they focus too heavily on one element while ignoring others. Some focus only on debt payoff and ignore investing. Others invest aggressively while maintaining high-interest debt. Some misuse credit and create instability. A successful system requires all components working together in harmony.

Risk management remains essential throughout the entire process. No financial system should assume perfect economic conditions. Income fluctuations, interest rate changes, emergencies, and market cycles must all be considered. Conservative planning ensures that acceleration does not come at the cost of financial fragility.

Another critical concept is scalability. A strong velocity banking system should work whether a household earns $4,000 per month or $40,000 per month. While higher income may accelerate results, the underlying system remains the same. Cash flow discipline, structured payments, liquidity management, and intentional spending are universal principles.

Emotional discipline continues to be one of the strongest predictors of success. Many financial systems fail not because they are mathematically incorrect, but because behavior breaks down over time. Consistency matters more than intensity. A moderately aggressive system maintained for years will outperform an aggressive system abandoned after a few months.

The ultimate blueprint also emphasizes adaptability. Life changes constantly. Careers evolve. Families grow. Businesses expand or contract. Economic conditions shift. A successful velocity banking system must adapt to these changes without collapsing. Flexibility ensures long-term sustainability.

One of the final stages of the system is financial independence transition. As mortgage balances decrease and investments grow, cash flow begins to exceed obligations significantly. At this stage, individuals gain options. They may choose to accelerate retirement, expand real estate portfolios, start businesses, reduce work hours, or pursue lifestyle changes that were previously impossible.

True financial freedom is not defined by a single paid-off mortgage. It is defined by the ability to make life decisions without being constrained by financial pressure. Velocity banking is simply one pathway that may help accelerate that outcome when implemented responsibly.

It is important to emphasize again that this system is not universally required for financial success. Many people build wealth through traditional investing, real estate strategies, entrepreneurship, or long-term disciplined savings. Velocity banking is simply one framework that combines debt reduction and cash flow optimization into a structured system.

The key takeaway from this entire series is control. Financial stress often comes from lack of control, not lack of income. When homeowners understand how money moves, how interest works, how credit functions, and how cash flow can be optimized, they gain the ability to make intentional decisions rather than reactive ones. The ultimate blueprint is not about complexity. It is about clarity. Every dollar has direction. Every decision has purpose. Every financial action contributes either to reducing debt, increasing liquidity, or building wealth. When these three elements work together consistently, financial acceleration becomes possible.

The system is simple in concept but powerful in execution:

- Understand your cash flow
- Protect your liquidity
- Reduce high-interest debt strategically
- Use credit intelligently, not emotionally
- Reinvest freed cash flow into wealth-building assets
- Maintain discipline consistently over time
- Adapt as life circumstances change

When applied consistently, this structure may transform financial outcomes over years and decades.

The mortgage does not have to define your financial life for 30 years. It can become a temporary phase that is strategically shortened, optimized, and integrated into a larger wealth-building plan.

That is the ultimate purpose of velocity banking.

Not just faster debt payoff.

But financial control, acceleration, and long-term freedom.

The Complete Velocity Banking Blueprint in Action

This example shows how the full velocity banking system works in real life. A homeowner has a $650,000 home with a $480,000 mortgage at 6.5% interest. Their monthly payment is about $3,035. Their household income is $12,500 per month, and after paying $6,000 in expenses and the mortgage, they still have about $3,465 left each month.

This creates strong monthly cash flow. Over a full year, that extra cash flow adds up to about $41,580. On top of that, the homeowner also receives an $18,000 annual bonus. Together, they have about $59,580 per year that can be used to accelerate mortgage payoff.

The homeowner uses this money strategically. They start by making a $60,000 lump "chunk" payment toward the mortgage, which reduces the balance from $480,000 to $420,000. Then they continue repeating this process each year by applying their surplus cash flow and bonuses toward the loan. This helps them pay off the mortgage in about 11–13 years instead of 30. Because the mortgage is paid off much faster, the homeowner avoids a large amount of interest. Instead of paying over $1,092,600 in total over 30 years (including about $612,600 in interest), they may reduce total interest to around $300,000. This creates estimated savings of more than $312,000.

After the mortgage is fully paid off, the homeowner now has an extra $3,035 per month in freed-up cash flow. Instead of going to the bank, this money can now be invested. If that amount is invested at an average 8% return for 20 years, it could grow to over $1.8 million.

The key lesson is that velocity banking is not just about paying off a mortgage faster. It is about using income, bonuses, and structured cash flow to reduce debt aggressively, save interest, and then redirect that freed-up money into investments. When used correctly and consistently, it can significantly accelerate both debt freedom and long-term wealth building.

Final Tips and Suggestions for Mortgage Freedom

From The Mortgage Payoff & Wealth Acceleration Series

Reaching mortgage freedom is not a single event—it is the result of consistent financial decisions, disciplined cash flow management, and a long-term commitment to controlling how money moves through your life. Across this entire series, you have seen different strategies: biweekly payments, lump sum reductions, refinancing optimization, velocity banking systems, rental income integration, and investment acceleration. Each method works differently, but they all share one truth: financial freedom is created through intentional structure, not random effort.

Before closing this series, it is important to step back and focus on the bigger picture. Mortgage freedom is not just about eliminating a loan. It is about creating flexibility, reducing financial stress, and unlocking the ability to choose how you live your life without being constrained by monthly debt obligations. The following final guidance is designed to help you consolidate everything you have learned into a practical, realistic, and sustainable long-term approach. One of the most important final principles is consistency over intensity. Many homeowners become highly motivated after learning about mortgage payoff strategies and attempt to make extreme financial changes all at once. They aggressively cut expenses, make large one-time payments, or restructure finances too quickly. While initial enthusiasm is helpful, long-term success depends on systems that can be maintained for years, not short bursts of effort followed by burnout.

Sustainable mortgage freedom comes from repeated behavior. Even small improvements—such as an extra monthly principal payment, a yearly lump sum, or improved budgeting—can create massive long-term results when applied consistently. The compounding effect of time is one of the most powerful forces in finance. A strategy that is simple and consistent will almost always outperform a strategy that is complex but unsustainable.

Another key principle is understanding that cash flow is more important than income alone. Many people believe that earning more money automatically solves financial problems. However, high income without control often leads to high expenses, increased debt, and ongoing financial pressure. True mortgage freedom is not about how much you earn—it is about how much you keep and how efficiently you use it.

Cash flow management means making intentional decisions about every dollar. It means avoiding lifestyle inflation, minimizing unnecessary debt, and directing surplus income toward strategic goals. Whether that goal is mortgage payoff, investing, or building reserves, cash flow discipline is the foundation that makes all other strategies work.

A third important concept is balance between debt reduction and liquidity. One of the most common mistakes homeowners make is becoming overly aggressive with mortgage payoff while ignoring emergency savings or financial flexibility. While paying off debt is valuable, removing all liquidity can create vulnerability. Unexpected expenses such as medical emergencies, job changes, or home repairs can quickly disrupt even the best financial plans.

A strong mortgage freedom strategy always includes reserves. Emergency savings act as financial protection and prevent you from relying on high-interest debt during unexpected situations. True financial strength is not just being debt-free—it is being debt-free and financially stable at the same time.

Another essential suggestion is to avoid emotional financial decisions. Money decisions are often influenced by stress, fear, excitement, or social pressure. People may rush into refinancing without understanding long-term costs, overspend after income increases, or delay financial action due to fear of making mistakes. Emotional decisions often lead to inconsistent results.

Mortgage freedom requires a calm, structured approach. Every financial decision should be evaluated based on long-term impact rather than short-term emotion. Before spending, borrowing, or investing, ask whether the decision supports your long-term financial direction or distracts from it. Over time, this simple habit creates powerful financial discipline.

It is also important to recognize that mortgage payoff is not always the final destination for everyone. Some homeowners benefit more from balancing mortgage reduction with investing, business growth, or real estate expansion. Others prioritize complete debt elimination for emotional peace and financial security. There is no single correct path. The best strategy is the one that aligns with your personal goals, risk tolerance, and lifestyle priorities.

For example, some individuals may choose to pay off their mortgage aggressively before investing heavily. Others may maintain a mortgage while building a diversified investment portfolio. Both approaches can lead to wealth when executed properly. The key is intentionality—not following a strategy blindly, but understanding why you are using it.

One of the most powerful long-term financial principles is opportunity awareness. Every dollar has a potential future value. Money used to pay down a mortgage early has a different long-term outcome than money invested in growth assets. Neither choice is inherently right or wrong, but understanding trade-offs is essential. Financial freedom comes from making informed decisions rather than emotional ones.

Another important suggestion is to periodically reassess your financial strategy. Life changes constantly—income shifts, family needs evolve, interest rates change, and economic conditions fluctuate. A strategy that made sense five years ago may not be optimal today. Reviewing your financial position at least once or twice per year ensures that your plan remains aligned with your current reality.

Flexibility is a hidden form of financial strength. The ability to adjust without panic or confusion is what separates financially stable households from those that struggle during change. Mortgage freedom is not about rigidity—it is about adaptability within a structured system.

Technology can also support long-term success. Budgeting tools, mortgage calculators, automated transfers, and financial tracking systems make it easier to stay consistent. Automation reduces emotional decision-making and ensures that positive financial habits continue even when life becomes busy or stressful. Another critical factor is education. Financial systems evolve, interest rates change, and new strategies emerge over time. Continuously learning about money, debt management, investing, and financial planning helps you stay ahead. The most financially successful individuals are not those who learn once—they are those who continue learning throughout their lives.

It is also important to maintain perspective. Mortgage freedom is a major achievement, but it should not come at the cost of life satisfaction. Financial discipline should improve your life, not restrict it entirely. There is a balance between enjoying the present and building for the future. A sustainable strategy allows for both.

Many people underestimate the emotional transformation that occurs when debt decreases. Stress often reduces, decision-making becomes easier, and life feels more flexible. These psychological benefits are just as important as the financial ones. Freedom is not only measured in numbers—it is also measured in peace of mind.

Another final tip is to focus on net worth, not just debt payoff. While eliminating a mortgage is powerful, true wealth is measured by total assets minus liabilities. A complete financial picture includes savings, investments, property value, business assets, and retirement accounts. Mortgage freedom should ideally be part of a larger wealth-building system rather than an isolated goal.

Ultimately, the most successful homeowners are those who think long-term. They understand that financial freedom is not created in months—it is built over years through consistent action. They avoid extreme decisions, stay disciplined during uncertain times, and remain focused on gradual improvement rather than instant results.

As you conclude this series, the most important takeaway is this: you already have the tools needed to change your financial future. The strategies in this series are not theoretical—they are practical systems that can be applied in real life. The difference between financial stress and financial freedom is not knowledge alone, but execution.

You do not need perfect timing. You do not need perfect income. You do not need perfect conditions. You need consistency, awareness, and commitment to long-term financial improvement.

Mortgage freedom is not just about eliminating a payment. It is about reclaiming control over your time, your choices, and your future. It is about creating a life where money supports your decisions rather than limiting them. The journey may take time, but every intentional financial decision brings you closer to that goal.

www.ingramcontent.com/pod-product-compliance
Ingram Content Group UK Ltd.
Pitfield, Milton Keynes, MK11 3LW, UK
UKHW010011031026
15589UKWH00008B/1606

9 798256 007553